THE DEAD SEA SCROLLS

A Short History

Weston W. Fields

BRILL

LEIDEN • BOSTON

THE DEAD SEA SCROLLS
A Short History

Weston W. Fields

ISBN-13: 978 90 04 15760 6
ISBN-10: 90 04 15760 3

Library of Congress Catalog Card Number: 2006937089

Other Photo Credits

Cover: Detail from the Great Isaiah Scroll (background), ©John C. Trever/Corbis*;*
    Inside Cave 4 at Qumran, ©James Whitmore, Time Life Pictures/Getty Images

pg 6, 8: Detail from Habakkuk Commentary Scroll, ©John C. Trever/Corbis

pg 104: Detail from Psalms Scroll, Courtesy of the IsraelAntiquities Authority/Bruce Zuckerman

Produced in cooperation with Publication Consultants

PO Box 221974 Anchorage, Alaska 99522-1974
books@publicationconsultants.com—www.publicationconsultants.com
Designed by Hal Gage, Gage Photo Graphics, halgage.com

Manufactured in the United States of America

DEDICATION

No one deserves more credit for the completion of this book and the forthcoming first
volume of the larger history than my wife,
Diane. For eight years she has been my
constant partner in this project down to the
minutest details. She assisted in almost all
the interviews on which much of this history
is based, and has lived out of a suitcase and
stayed more nights in hotels for more years
than anyone can be reasonably expected to
endure. This book is for you, Diane.

TABLE OF CONTENTS

ACKNOWLEDGMENTS

Many friends, old and new, have co-operated in amassing the vast collection of materials used in the forthcoming complete history of the Dead Sea Scrolls on which this short history is based. The complete history will contain full documentation of interviews, other sources, and a more exhaustive list of those who assisted, but for now, I want to thank those who aided the most, or who worked directly on this book.

My colleague of many years at the Dead Seas Scrolls Foundation in Jerusalem, Mrs. Eva Ben-David, has helped at all stages of the larger volume and this one as well. Her facility in five languages has been invaluable: translator of documents, phone calls to scholars in many countries, translator during some of the interviews, capable researcher, proofreader, general facilitator, confidant and friend.

I am indebted to Prof. Shemaryahu Talmon and Prof. Emanuel Tov of the Hebrew University of Jerusalem, who initiated me into the world of the Dead Sea Scrolls more than twenty years ago. Profs. Frank M. Cross and John Strugnell of Harvard hosted Diane and me several times in Boston, and Prof. Cross has not only taken frequent telephone calls and replied to many e-mails, but he has read the first volume of the larger work and suggested corrections and changes. Józef and Yolanta Milik gave freely of their time in more than a dozen interviews in Paris. John and Elizabeth Trever welcomed us into their home in California on several occasions. Likewise, Prof. James Sanders of Claremont granted several interviews and has read the first volume of the larger book. Prof. David Noel Freedman of San Diego provided invaluable information and help in numerous conversations, interviews and letters.

Many others willingly consented to interviews as well—some even three or four times: Prof. C.-H. Hunzinger in Hamburg, Profs. Geza Vermeś and P. Wernberg-Møller in Oxford, Prof. Henri de Contenson in Paris, Fr. Dominque Barthélemy in Fribourg, Switzerland, Prof. A. Van der Woude in Groningen and Fr. J. P. M. van der Ploeg in Nijmegen, the Netherlands, Fr. Joseph Fitzmyer in Washington, DC, Prof. David Flusser and Anton Hazou in Jerusalem, HRH Prince El Hassan bin Talal at the Royal Palace in Amman, and Dr. Razi Bisheh, also in Amman.

Fr. Emile Puech of the École Biblique et Archéologique Française de Jérusalem helped me obtain material and gave advice. Fr. Marcel Sigrist, also at the École Biblique, made the original suggestion of recording the oral history concerning the scrolls, the impetus for the entire project.

Pnina Shor and Ruta Peled at the Israel Antiquities Authority in Jerusalem helped secure permission to copy the entire archive concerning the scrolls from the Palestine Archaeological Museum (now the Rockefeller Museum). Joan Allegro hosted us twice on the Isle of Man and allowed me to copy her late husband's archive. Judith Allegro Brown sent a pre-publication manuscript of her recent book about her father. Martha Brownlee Terry provided photographs and permitted us to copy her father's archive at the University of Manchester. Prof. George Brooke copied and sent it. Fr. Joseph Jensen, Fr. Sidney Griffiths, and Dr. Monica Blanchard at the Catholic University of America in Washington, DC, helped find the Skehan Archive.

Prof. Esther Chazon at the Hebrew University of Jerusalem gave me access to the archives at the Orion Center for Dead Sea Scrolls Research, and Magen Broshi, formerly Director of the Shrine of the Book in Jerusalem was always ready to answer questions or help suggest places to look for documents. Prof. Eric Myers of Duke University sent items from the archives of the American Schools of Oriental Research. Dr. George Kiraz provided a pre-publication manuscript of his book containing his father's personal papers. William Kando met me many times and freely related his family's traditions and stories.

Pnina Shor and Yael Barshek at the Israel Antiquities Authority in Jerusalem generously provided photographs, as did James Trever (John's son), Prof. Bruce Zuckerman of the University of Southern California and the West Semitic Research Project, together with Ken Zuckerman and Dr. Marilyn Lundberg. Fr. Jean-Michel de Tarragon at the École Biblique in Jerusalem provided photos and, together with Fr. Jean-Baptiste Humbert, helped me find the de Vaux archive.

Dr. Davina Eisenberg of Cape Town, South Africa and I translated many French documents together, particularly letters of Père (Father) de Vaux and all the French introductions to the volumes of Discoveries in the Judaean Desert (DJD). Her father, Dr. Isaac Eisenberg, read the entire manuscript and made suggestions. Nadia Elkebir of Cape Town and Paris also helped translate some of de Vaux's letters. My close friend of many years, Dan Earle of Seattle and Kodiak, read the manuscript and suggested changes which improved it considerably. Ms. Lorna Hiles of Oxford University Press in Cape Town checked style. Hans van der Meij and Mattie Kuiper of Brill Academic Publishers in Leiden, the Netherlands, guided, encouraged, and suggested improvements. Evan Swensen of Publication Consultants and Hal Gage of Gage Photo Graphics, both in Anchorage, Alaska, were responsible for the final design and production. Rebecca Goodrich of Ghostwriter, also in Anchorage, Alaska, rendered the final proofing and editing. Curtis Hight provided assistance with Hebrew fonts and programming.

The Dead Sea region. ©Brian Firestone/Shutterstock

PREFACE

This book is meant to give non-specialists a convenient and updated summary of the history of the scrolls, their relationship to Judaism and Christianity, and their importance for understanding how the Bible was passed down from generation to generation. It is meant to supplement the small amount of information it is possible to convey in an exhibition, a magazine article or a television program, and at the same time serve as an introduction into the larger world of the Dead Sea Scrolls.

The photographs include samples of some of the largest and most well-known scrolls. A few of these will coincide with scrolls displayed in exhibitions now taking place or planned. Others portray scrolls that have seldom traveled outside Israel or Jordan.

The history of the scrolls offered here will serve as an introduction to a much larger work, my forthcoming two-volume history of the Dead Sea Scrolls. The larger book is based mainly on two new sources of information: first, more than forty interviews with the men who discovered, excavated, and were the first scholars to decipher and edit the scrolls, and second, several archives of personal letters and papers, most of which have never been published.

The Great Isaiah Scroll (1QIsaᵃ), Column 8 lines 23-26
(Isaiah 9:6, 7 from the *Jerusalem Bible*)

23 (Is 9:6) For there is a child born for us, a son given to us and dominion is laid

24 on his shoulders; and this is the name they give him: Wonder-Counsellor, Mighty-God, Eternal-Father, Prince of Peace. (Is 9:7) Wide

25 is his dominion in a peace that has no end, for the throne of David and for his royal power, which he establishes and makes secure

26 in justice and integrity. From this time onwards and for ever, the jealous love of Yahweh Sabaoth will do this.

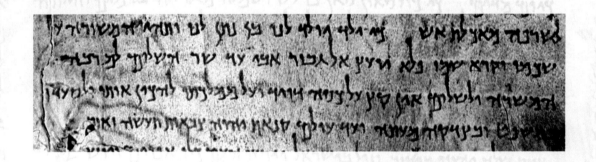

The escarpment containing Qumran Cave 4. Alistair Duncan/Dorling Kinndersley/Getty Images

Chapter 1

DISCOVERY AND PURCHASE
OF THE DEAD SEA SCROLLS

From the left, Muhammed ed-Dib and Jum'a at the entrance to Cave 1, Qumran. Courtesy of the *École Biblique et Archéologique Française de Jérusalem*

Qumran, Cave 1: 1947-49

The first three Dead Sea Scrolls were accidentally discovered close to the northwest shore of the Dead Sea in a cave near Khirbet Qumran in about January-February of 1947 by three Bedouin shepherds: Muhammed "ed-Dib (the wolf)" Ahmad el-Hamid, Jum'a Muhammed Khalil, and Khalil Musa. By March, Jum'a and Khalil had shown the scrolls (the Great Isaiah Scroll, the Habakkuk Commentary, and the Manual of Discipline in two pieces) to several people in Bethlehem: Ibrahim 'Ijha, George Isha'ya, and Khalil Iskander Shahin (Kando), the latter an antiquities dealer.

During Easter Week George mentioned the scrolls to the Metropolitan Mar Athanasius Samuel, Archbishop of the Syrian Orthodox Church, who lived at St. Mark's Monastery in Jerusalem's Old City. Both George and Kando were members of the Syrian Church. Samuel asked George to contact the Bedouin and find out more about the scrolls. He also telephoned the Syrian merchant in Bethlehem (Kando), and urged him to get the scrolls "by all means."

By June, Jum'a and the enterprising George had returned to Qumran, and removed four more scrolls. Three of these (Isaiah[b], the War Scroll, and the Thanksgiving Scroll) were eventually, but not immediately,

17

sold for £7 to Faidi Salahi in Bethlehem. Kando later ended up with the fourth, the Genesis Apocryphon (Lamech Scroll).

Anxious to find a buyer, Kando advised Jum'a, Khalil Musa, and George to present all seven of their scrolls to Mar Samuel in Jeru-

The opening to Cave 1, Qumran. © John C. Trever

salem on July 5, 1947, but they were rudely turned away from St. Mark's Monastery by Fr. Boulos Jilf (Gilf), who knew neither who they were, nor the value of what they carried in their hands. Jum'a and George took their three scrolls (Isaiah[b], War Scroll, Thanksgiving Scroll), Khalil took the other three (Isaiah[a], Habakkuk Commentary, Manual of Discipline in two pieces), and, apparently, Khalil gave the Genesis Apocryphon to George and Jum'a. It would be many years before all seven scrolls were together again in the same place at the same time.

During the next few days Kando agreed to sell the four scrolls held by Jum'a and George (Isaiah[a], Habakkuk Commentary, Manual of Discipline in two pieces, and the Genesis Apocryphon) in exchange for a commission of one-third of whatever he could obtain. Kando accompanied George and two Bedouin to St. Mark's Monastery, where they left their four scrolls in the care of Mar Samuel. As yet, no one fully appreciated the value of what they had, least of all Kando. Eventually, he would sell these four scrolls to Mar Samuel for £24 (Palestine pounds = US $97.20), saying, "much dirty paper for little clean paper." Of this amount Kando gave two-thirds, (£16 = US $64.80) to the Bedouin, as they had previously agreed. But in July 1947 neither Samuel nor Kando yet knew exactly what these ancient documents were.

Over the next several months Samuel repeatedly attempted to obtain independent scholarly confirmation of their age and information about their content, with no success whatsoever. He invited two Dominican specialists in Syriac, Frs. Van der Ploeg and Marmadji, to examine the "Big Scroll." Although Fr. Van der Ploeg identified it as Isaiah (which Samuel had not yet known), neither was a specialist in ancient Hebrew writing styles, so its great antiquity escaped them.

As the hot Palestinian summer waxed strong, Samuel once more sent George, accompanied by the Bedouin, back to the "scroll cave." They found more evidence of occupation and storage: pieces of cloth wrappings, broken scroll jars, and even one unbroken jar.

Day by day, week by week, Samuel continued to consult various scholars about the age of the four scrolls Kando had entrusted to him. Stephan Hanna Stephan of the Transjordan Department of Antiquities pronounced them "late" (medieval). Some Jerusalem scholars who were invited to look at them didn't even take the story seriously enough to come to St. Mark's.

Finally, having given up on the Jerusalem scholarly community, Mar Samuel left on September 15, 1947 for Homs, Syria with Anton Kiraz, another Syrian Orthodox merchant in Jerusalem, as his driver. In Homs he showed the scrolls to Mar Ignatius Ephram 1, Syrian Orthodox Patriarch of Antioch. Like all the others until now, he also doubted their antiquity, suggesting they were no more than three or four hundred years old. The Patriarch advised Samuel, however, to show them to the Professor of Hebrew at the American University of Beirut; but when Samuel arrived in Beirut the Professor was away on vacation.

Back in Jerusalem, Samuel continued his quest. The next visitor to St. Mark's was a Jewish specialist in Hebrew antiquities, Toviah Wechsler. Although he did not recognize the Scrolls' antiquity, he did understand their potential value if they were as old as the Archbishop Samuel suspected. "Your Grace," Wechsler is reported to have said, "if these came from the time of Christ as you imply, you couldn't begin to measure their value by filling a box the size of this [large] table with pounds sterling."

By the first week of October nearly six months had elapsed since the Archbishop Samuel had first heard about the scrolls. About this time Kiraz and Samuel became partners in the scrolls in return for Kiraz's financial support. Like many business partnerships, it was to prove less than fully satisfactory.

The parade of outsiders viewing the ancient documents at St. Mark's continued. Dr. Maurice Brown, a Jewish physician, made a call to Samuel to discuss the matter of a vacant building adjacent to the Syrian Orthodox School on Prophets Street in West Jerusalem. Since he was Jewish, Samuel assumed that he might be able help date or identify them. While Brown himself could not help Samuel with dating the scrolls, he said he knew someone who could. Samuel later learned that Brown called the President of the Hebrew University of Jerusalem, Dr. Judah L. Magnes, who sent two men from the University library staff to see the scrolls a few weeks later, probably still in October 1947. "When they came," Samuel writes, "they spoke Hebrew to each other, and they said that it would be necessary for them to consult their specialist at the Hebrew University before they could make any kind of a statement." The librarians asked if they could take photographs, and Samuel consented, on condition that they returned and took the photographs at St. Mark's. They never returned. Brown also sent Yoav Sasson, a well-known Jewish antiquities dealer in the Old City, to Samuel. He suggested, after seeing the scrolls, that Samuel should send them

Prof. Eleazar L. Sukenik studying the War Scroll in Jerusalem, 1950. Bettmann/Corbis

to experts in Europe, but the Archbishop wisely declined.

More weeks went by. All during August, September and October there had been no word about the other three scrolls (Isaiah[b], The War Scroll, and the Thanksgiving Scroll), the ones removed by George and Jum'a from the "first cave" sometime after the initial discovery. Suddenly parts of two of these showed up in the hands of an Armenian antiquities dealer, Nasri Ohan.

At the beginning of the Jewish work week on Sunday, November 23, Ohan ("Mr. X" in the original account) contacted Prof Eleazar L. Sukenik, Professor of Archaeology at the Hebrew University of Jerusalem, a specialist in Hebrew epigraphy and the archaeology of ancient synagogues. Ohan and Sukenik were long-time friends. The call to meet once again was unusual only because of the political circumstances at the time. Jerusalem was divided into different areas, and one needed a pass to enter each. Since Sukenik did not have the proper pass they had their meeting across a barbed wire fence at the gateway to Military Zone B.

Through the fence Ohan related that one of their mutual friends, an old Arab antiquities dealer in Bethlehem, had come to him the previous day with a rather strange tale. Some Bedouin had called on this Bethlehem dealer, bringing with them several parchment scrolls which they claimed to have found in a cave near the shores of the Dead Sea, not far from Jericho. These they had offered to sell to him, but the dealer did not know whether they were genuine, nor did he have any idea of what was written on them or how old they were. The Bethlehem dealer had therefore brought samples to Ohan, probably because he knew that from time to time Ohan had sold antiquities to the

Department of Archaeology and its museum at the Hebrew University. But Ohan, too, had no knowledge of whether they were really ancient manuscripts or a relatively recent product. He wanted to know from Sukenik whether he considered them genuine, and if so, whether he would be prepared to buy them for the Museum of Jewish Antiquities of the Hebrew University.

As he peered at the samples, Sukenik at first thought they might be forgeries, but then he recognized similarities between the letters on the scrolls and those he had seen on small coffins for bones (ossuaries) which he had discovered in ancient tombs in and near Jerusalem, dating to the period before the destruction of the Temple in 70 CE (AD). He had seen such letters scratched, carved and, in a few cases, painted on stone. But not until then had he seen this particular kind of Hebrew lettering written with a pen on parchment.

It did not take Sukenik long to decide he wanted the scrolls, but ever conscious of maintaining a good bargaining position, he made no indication. He asked Ohan to proceed at once to Bethlehem, bring back more samples, and telephone him when he returned. In the meantime Sukenik would obtain a military pass so that he could visit

Ohan at his store and examine the parchments more closely.

On Thursday, November 27, Ohan tele-

Prof. Eleazar L. Sukenik studying the Thanksgiving Scroll in Jerusalem, January 1, 1950. Houlton Archive/Getty Images

phoned to say that he had some additional fragments. Sukenik "raced over" to see him. He sat in Ohan's store and tried to decipher the writing. He was now more convinced than ever that these were fragments of genuine ancient scrolls. They resolved to go together to Bethlehem to start negotiations with the Arab dealer for their purchase. The next day they intended to go to Bethlehem, but Sukenik's wife and son, Yigael Yadin, dissuaded him in view of the danger. Later that evening he heard on the radio that the

United Nations, expected to vote that day on the partition of Palestine into Jewish and Arab territories, had postponed its decision. Sukenik believed that Arab attacks would begin immediately after the vote, so he resolved to make the journey the next morning, and this time tell neither his wife nor son. The next day was the Sabbath, but Sukenik and Ohan took a bus to Bethlehem, where they

Part of the "Thanksgiving Scroll" (Hodayot) fragment purchased by Sukenik in 1947. Hulton Archive/Getty Images

proceeded directly to the home of the antiquities dealer, Feidi Salahi. After considerable bargaining, Salahi allowed Sukenik to take the scrolls home for further examination. Sukenik promised to let him know within two days, through Ohan, whether he would purchase them.

As soon as Sukenik got home he began his examination, but he could not identify the texts. That evening he called on several colleagues for advice, but none could help. The next morning, Sunday, he was com-

pletely certain he would purchase them, but it was Ohan's day of rest, so it was Monday, December 1, 1947 before he was able to telephone his Armenian friend, and instruct him to inform Salahi that he did, indeed, want the scrolls.

While Sukenik had been examining the scrolls in his study that Saturday night, the late news on the radio announced that the United Nations would be voting on the resolution for the partition of Palestine (November 29, 1947). While he was working, his son rushed in, shouting that the vote in favor of the Jewish State had been carried. As Sukenik later wrote, "This great event in Jewish history was thus combined in my home in Jerusalem with another event, no less historic, the one political, the other cultural."

Dr. Magnes made available the initial funds needed for purchasing the scrolls. We do not have a record of how, when, or where the money was exchanged, but it was probably sent through Ohan on December 1 or 2.

Shortly afterwards, one of the librarians at the Hebrew University who had seen one or more of the St. Mark's scrolls happened to see Sukenik and told him about the incident, saying he had tried to follow up, but had been unsuccessful in re-contacting Mar Samuel. Sukenik could not enter the Old

City to check this story himself, but a few days later he received a telephone call from Ohan telling him he hoped to obtain more scrolls from the same source soon.

The problem of money began to worry Sukenik. He knew it might take considerable funds to purchase further scrolls. He therefore asked his bank for a personal loan of £1,500, and offered his small house in Rehavia as surety. This arrangement was accepted by the bank, and Sukenik was given the necessary papers to fill out; but he was persuaded by friends to forego the personal loan, and did not follow through.

With the British withdrawal from Palestine looming, the political situation continued to deteriorate. Sukenik urged Ohan to continue his efforts to obtain more of these scrolls from the Bedouin. He had no way of knowing, of course, that the group of scrolls he had already agreed to buy, together with those he now knew were at St. Mark's, comprised the sum total of all scrolls found so far, apart from a few other fragments. He enlisted the help of Dr. James Bieberkraut, a refugee from Germany and an expert in this sort of work, to help him unroll the scrolls. As they worked together, Sukenik was able to read them, identifying what later came to be known as the War Scroll and the Thanksgiving Scroll (*Hodayot*).

On December 22, 1947 Sukenik purchased more scroll fragments from the Bethlehem dealer Salahi, through Ohan: Salahi's third scroll (Isaiah[b] and possibly some Daniel and other biblical fragments as well). The other four scrolls were still across town from

Sukenik in the Old City, and Sukenik had not yet seen them.

Weeks passed and then, without warning, toward the end of January 1948, Sukenik received a letter from an acquaintance in the Arab Quarter, Anton Kiraz. A member of the Syrian Orthodox Christian Community, as we have said, Kiraz was the owner of the property near Talpiot in South Jerusalem, where Sukenik and his colleague Nahum Avigad had two years earlier discovered an ancient Jewish tomb dating from the first century CE. As Mar Samuel's "partner" in the scrolls (unbeknown to Sukenik), Kiraz divulged to Sukenik that he had in his possession some ancient Hebrew scrolls he wished to show him. They decided to meet at the beautiful YMCA building in West Jerusalem, a comfortable and accessible meeting spot, often so used by Jerusalemites, even today. They met in the office of the librarian, Malak Tannourdji, also a member of the Syrian community.

To this meeting Kiraz brought Isaiah[a], the Manual of Discipline, the Habakkuk Commentary, and the Genesis Apocryphon, indicating that together with Mar Samuel, he was co-owner of these scrolls. But Sukenik had no way of knowing the full truth about all the dealings between Kiraz, Samuel, the Bedouin, and Kando, nor did he know that the scrolls he had already purchased from Salahi had been brought to St. Mark's the previous July 5 when the Bedouin were abruptly turned away without an audience.

Kiraz asked Sukenik's opinion about their age and authenticity. Sukenik replied he

William Brownlee studying photographs of scroll fragments, early 1950s. Courtesy of Martha Brownlee Terry

considered them quite ancient, and he would be willing to buy them for the Hebrew University. But he requested that he be allowed to take them home for examination. With a promise to return the scrolls to Kiraz in a few days' time, Sukenik left the YMCA with Isaiah[a], one part of the Manual of Discipline and the Habakkuk Commentary in hand. The other part of the Manual and the Genesis Apocryphon were kept by Tannourdji in his desk drawer.

During the ensuing days Sukenik read what he could of the scrolls and showed them as well to Magnes and two university colleagues. Day and night he returned to the manuscripts, sometimes even rising in the wee hours of the morning to read them. The Isaiah Scroll interested him particularly, and he copied several of its chapters.

Increasingly worried about the amount of money it would take to buy this second batch, Sukenik estimated that two thousand pounds sterling would be sufficient. He began to cast about for a source. He returned to his bank to claim the loan he had been promised, but the political and military situation was by then so grim he was refused. Sukenik now bitterly regretted that he had permitted himself to be dissuaded from raising that loan earlier. He intended to turn for help to the Bialik Foundation, the literary arm of the Jewish Agency, but a conflict of schedules made it impossible for him to meet the proper authorities before he had to return the scrolls to Kiraz. To this end they met once more at the YMCA on Friday, February 6, 1948. Both wanted to bargain for the purchase. Sukenik offered £100, but Kiraz showed no interest. Stubbornly, they both held out.

A third meeting on February 10 went no further. Sukenik raised the offer to £500, plus a commission of another £500 for Kiraz himself. This offer was likewise rejected. When they both realized that they had come to an impasse, they agreed to meet again at the Yugoslav Consulate, where the gatekeeper was a Syrian friend of Kiraz, but only after Kiraz had confirmed the meeting in writing. Sukenik later wrote, "I walked home slowly. The deserted streets fitted my mood of empty depression."

John Trever in Jerusaslem, 1947–1948. © John C. Trever

No sooner had Sukenik walked in the door than representatives of the Bialik Foundation arrived to see the scrolls. He showed them some fragments from his first purchases. Excited, they promised to bring the matter to the attention of Ben-Gurion (future first Prime Minister of Israel). A few days later Sukenik was informed that the Jewish Agency/Bialik Foundation was willing to put up any sums needed for the purchase of the scrolls, but weeks passed without news from Kiraz. Despite repeated attempts to see the scrolls again or at least negotiate for their purchase, he was never able to do either. Eventually, Sukenik received a letter informing him that Kiraz and Samuel had decided not to sell. Sukenik was crushed. Their story was that "they preferred to wait until the world was once again open to them, and they could find out the market price." It was some time before Sukenik was to discover what had really happened, and Sukenik died in 1953, still believing that these scrolls he had held in his hands were lost to the Jewish people forever.

Meanwhile the situation in Arab East Jerusalem and the Old City was getting more desperate. Skirmishes among Arabs, Jews, and the British were rampant. Some students at the American School of Oriental Research (ASOR; today, the Albright Institute of Archaeology) had not returned after the semester break, although two young American post-doctoral fellows at the school, William Brownlee (Ph.D., Duke) and John Trever (Ph.D., Yale), had decided to remain. The Annual Director of the American School, Prof. Millar Burrows of Yale, had left on a short expedition to Iraq on Sunday, February 15. The stage was set for a radical turn of events, but none of the players yet knew it.

Mar Samuel later claimed he did not know that his partner, Kiraz, had been negotiating with Sukenik in West Jerusalem, though he must have known. For his part, he was looking for a buyer as well. On February 17 he requested that Kiraz return the scrolls to St. Mark's.

Samuel's assistant, the Rev. Fr. Butros Sowmy, recalled having visited the American School some ten years before. He especially remembered the cordial welcome he had received, and suggested to the Archbishop Samuel that he might obtain some kind of help with dating and identifying the scrolls there.

On Wednesday, February 18 Brownlee decided to go shopping for wrapping paper so he could begin packaging certain belongings he might have to send out of the country at a moment's notice (due to the volatile political situation). Before leaving on his mission early that afternoon he had had a strange premonition that he should not leave. He knelt down and prayed in his small room on the second floor of the School, feeling that perhaps it was not safe for him to venture out, but he received assurance that it would be safe, so he departed.

At about 4:30 that afternoon, Fr. Sowmy telephoned the American School. The School cook, Omar, answered. Sowmy asked for Brownlee, who had been recommended by someone at St. George's Anglican Cathedral, just down the road from the American School. He was not in his room. Brownlee's premonition had been correct, but for a different reason. The Director, Burrows, was gone, so Omar called another of the annual fellows, Trever, acting Director in Burrows' absence.

Sowmy and Mar Samuel had fabricated a story that was only later unmasked. Sowmy told Trever that as librarian of St. Mark's Monastery he was in the process of organizing its rare books, and had found some scrolls in ancient Hebrew which had been at the monastery for about forty years (similar to the story told to the librarians from Hebrew University some months before). He wanted to have more information on them, and wondered whether Trever would be willing take a look.

Brownlee did not return until supper time. At supper he overheard Trever talking about the telephone call he had received, and the strange claim of a Syrian monk that St. Mark's Monastery had ancient scrolls going back to the time of Christ in its possession. Trever also mentioned an appointment to see the documents the next day. Although he was skeptical about the claimed antiquity of the scrolls, Trever judged it wise to look into the matter. Brownlee heard enough to know the telephone call had been intended for him, and he naturally wanted to see the scrolls as well.

Trever had invited Sowmy to return to the School the following day, February 19, at 2:30 p.m. Sowmy arrived with his brother, Ibrahim, a customs official for the Mandate Government. But Trever had left his camera at the Palestine Archaeological Museum the previous day, so he couldn't photograph the scrolls: he was reduced to copying by hand a few lines from the Isaiah Scroll for further study. After an hour, the two Sowmy brothers left, taking the scrolls with them.

Having decided to run some errands before the scrolls appeared, Brownlee had missed out on the meeting again because he thought they were coming at 3:30 whereas they came at 2:30. Upon his return he discovered the two Syrians had come and gone. Trever showed Brownlee two lines of text which he had copied from the largest roll. Brownlee made a copy of the transcription and went to work independently on the deciphering and identification. About ten minutes later Trever burst into Brownlee's room with the thrilling announcement that he had identified the passage as Isaiah 65:1-2. It was sometime afterward, Trever relates, that the irony of the first verse impressed itself upon him:

I am sought of them that asked not for me;

I am found of them that sought me not! (*King James Version*)

But to Brownlee the scroll had said something different:

I was ready to be sought by those who did not ask for me;

I was *ready to be found* by those who did not seek me! (*Revised Standard Version*)

As far as they knew, they were the first scholars to learn of the spectacular discovery. Trever soon thought to make a comparison between the text of the scroll and a photo of the Nash Papyrus, a document which Prof. W. F. Albright of Johns Hopkins University had dated back to about *100 BCE (BC)*, consisting of a single leaf containing in Hebrew the Ten Commandments and the *Shema* ("Hear, O Israel, the LORD our God is one").

But what to do next? Trever and Brownlee realized that these documents must be photographed, especially in light of the rapidly deteriorating political situation in the city. So on Friday, February 20, just two days after his first phone call from Sowmy, Trever set out for St. Mark's Monastery in the Old City, by way of Jaffa Gate. Trever was greeted at the monastery by Fr. Sowmy, who introduced him to His Grace, the Metropolitan (Archbishop) Athanasius Yeshue Samuel. Getting permission to photograph the scrolls was not easy, but Trever finally persuaded Samuel by arguing that the better known the scrolls became, the more they would be worth.

With the rather meager equipment at hand, Trever and Brownlee began making preparations early the next day for the visit of the Syrians. They set up in the basement. Brownlee tells the story: "We were alarmed by the fact that there was no electricity as yet [due to the near collapse of East Jerusalem's power infrastructure], so we were prepared for either eventuality: to use daylight or to work more conveniently under electric flood lights. I changed the roll in my movie camera so as to get a picture of the Syrians when they arrived with the scrolls, and Trever was prepared to meet them at the gate of the school yard."

The Syrians arrived promptly at 9:30 a.m. This time the Metropolitan Samuel himself accompanied Sowmy. They all went to the basement. It seemed portentous to them that just as they were to begin photographing, the lights suddenly came back on. They started with the Isaiah Scroll, measuring about twenty-four feet long and ten inches high, consisting of seventeen sheets or strips of skin sewed end to end. The text was distributed into fifty-four columns. Brownlee held the scroll flat while Trever used the camera. That first day they finished the entire Isaiah Scroll and a smaller scroll Brownlee had been able to identify as a commentary on the biblical book of Habakkuk. By February 25 Trever had prints ready, and he air-mailed these from Jerusalem to Prof. Albright in Baltimore.

John Trever photographing the Great Isaiah Scroll, 1948. © *John C. Trever*

of the year should be devoted largely to the study of their recently found documents.

Over the next few days Brownlee, Trever and Burrows spent as much time as possible on the scrolls, though a good bit of Trever's time was taken up by negotiations with the Syrians. Still, they came to a few important conclusions at this early stage: one scroll was indeed a commentary on Habakkuk, another was a manual for the behavior of a Jewish sect or group of some sort, the group resembled the ancient Jewish Essene sect as described by the first century Jewish historian Josephus, and the Isaiah scroll had important textual variants from the traditional or Masoretic text.

When the photographs arrived at John

Full of stories about his trips to ancient Ur and Babylon, Burrows returned from Baghdad on February 28. Trever and Brownlee were just as keen to tell their stories of the past ten days' events and begin to spill them out. Ever the cautious scholar, Burrows urged the two young men to be careful not to jump to conclusions prematurely, but he agreed that their classes for the remainder

Inner courtyard of the Palestine Archaeological Museum. Courtesy of the Israel Antiquities Authority

Hopkins University, Prof. Albright could hardly contain himself. As Prof. Frank M. Cross relates:

> One day in the spring of 1948, Noel Freedman and I were working in our carrels in the Johns Hopkins library when Professor William F. Albright, our teacher, came rushing into the library. He herded us into his study and whipped out glossy prints of manuscript columns received from John Trever in Jerusalem. The text was from Isaiah. He dated the Isaiah scroll before our eyes, explaining the typologically significant features of the script.

Fr. Roland de Vaux, O.P. Courtesy of the École Biblique et Archéologique

With a few minutes' study he was able to assign the manuscript to the second century BCE. It was a remarkable performance. But Albright was prepared. In 1937, he had published his classic analysis of the Nash Papyrus, organizing the field in the process, and by 1947, he had gathered a large amount of additional data bearing on the topology of the Aramaic and Jewish scripts of this era, planning an updating of his earlier paper.

Finally, in early March, the Syrians disclosed to Trever that the discovery of the scrolls had been recent, not forty years in the past. Of course the Syrians themselves did not know exactly when the scrolls had been discovered, and apparently it was not even completely clear to them that there had been two entirely separate groups, possibly indicating two separate discoveries. But at least Trever, Brownlee, and Burrows now knew that the discovery had been in the recent, not distant, past (1946 or 1947, not 40 years before).

This brought up a new problem. Now that they knew the discovery to be recent, that is, within the time period of the thirty-one years of the British Mandate (1917-1948), not during the time of the Ottoman Empire (preceding 1917), "there was a legal obligation" on their part, Brownlee relates, "to inform the Department of Antiquities to this effect."

However, this led to a further problem, a difficult question often arising when one is acting as the middleman between antiquities dealers and antiquities authorities: how much does one reveal about his sources to either side? As Brownlee understood, speaking to the Antiquities Department might be seen as "assuming the role of the informer against the Syrians, which Trever and Burrows were loathe to do." They also worried that if they did report the discovery to the authorities, the scrolls would be seized and stored in the Palestine Archaeological Museum, which, situated as it was in East Jerusalem only a few blocks from West Jerusalem, was likely to be in the midst of the fighting everyone knew would soon erupt into war. (As it turned out, the Museum was not damaged significantly in the war.)

Meanwhile, Trever was not satisfied with the negatives he had made of the Isaiah Scroll, so he asked the Syrians to lend him the scroll again, and allow him to keep it at the American School so he could produce a new set. It was this set he published a few years later.

On March 15, 1948 Trever finally received the answer he had been awaiting from Albright. Albright agreed the scrolls predated the time of Jesus. "My heartiest congratulations," Albright wrote, "on the greatest manuscript discovery of modern times! There is no doubt in my mind that the script is more archaic than that of the Nash Papyrus …. I should prefer a date around 100 BCE…. What an absolutely incredible find! And there can happily not be the slightest doubt in the world about the genuineness of the manuscript."

As Trever met again and again with the Syrians he also discovered, to his great disappointment, that he and Brownlee had not been the first to identify the Isaiah scroll. Fr.

Excavating Qumran Cave 1, 1949. From the left, G.W.L. Harding and R. de Vaux. Harding is using a sifter to filter out small fragments of scrolls from the dirt on the cave's floor. © John C. Trever

Van der Ploeg had identified its content in July 1947 and Sukenik had recognized its great antiquity more than two weeks before they saw it.

Throughout March, Trever continued to go back and forth to St. Mark's almost daily. On one of his visits he noticed that part of the "fourth scroll" (Genesis Apocryphon) was becoming more pliable and peeling off the roll. He separated it from the roll and was able to identify the language as Aramaic, the same language written on a piece he suspected had broken off earlier. He was permitted to bring it back to the American school where he photographed it, still rolled up, in black and white and in color.

With war impending, the Metropolitan Samuel, accompanied by Fr. Sowmy, left Jerusalem with the scrolls on the morning of March 25. He did not inform his partner Kiraz. Traveling by way of Homs, Syria, to report on the dire financial and social situation of the Syrian Christians in Palestine, they arrived in Beirut, where they deposited the scrolls in a vault for safekeeping. There the scrolls remained until the very end of 1948.

An announcement concerning the scrolls had been composed by Burrows, approved by Samuel, and mailed from Jerusalem three weeks earlier. Now Yale University released

Yusef Saad at the main entrance to the Palestine Archaeological Museum. In the background, Mt. Scopus and the tower of Augusta Victoria church and hospital on the ridge leading to the Mount of Olives to the left. Courtesy of the Israel Antiquities Authority

it on April 10 for publication in the Sunday papers the following day. One can only imagine Sukenik's dismay when he saw the Yale University press release in which Burrows and Samuel seemed to have deliberately misled the public. For four months he had sat on his own purchase of three scrolls (Isaiah[b], the War Scroll, and the Thanksgiving Scroll), as well as his examination of parts of the others (Isaiah[a] and part of the Manual of Discipline) before Trever and Brownlee had seen them. In order to counter the misinformation he broke his silence in his own press release on April 26.

Shortly after midnight on May 14, 1948 the British withdrew from Jerusalem. The next day, Sowmy was struck in the head and killed by shrapnel while standing in the courtyard of St. Mark's Monastery. Once Israel's War of Independence began, it was anyone's guess who would finally end up in control of Qumran. It was more difficult than ever to get back and forth from the Judean desert to Bethlehem or Jerusalem. The Bedouin were frequently there, of course, because they moved across the invisible borders at will, but "city Arabs" ventured there less often, unaccustomed to the harsh environment and unprepared as they were, for "living off the land" like the Bedouin.

The discovery and a description of the scrolls was first presented to the scholarly world in the September 1948 issue of the *Biblical Archaeologist*, followed by articles in October 1948 and February 1949 in the *Bulletin of the American Schools of Oriental Research*. Also in September 1948 Sukenik published in Hebrew a preliminary survey of the Hebrew University scrolls, excerpts from the texts, and a transcription of chapters forty-two and forty-three of Isaiah[a], proving that he had seen it before Trever and Brownlee. In doing so, however, he seems to have violated the exclusive right of publication conferred by Samuel upon the American Schools. But from Sukenik's point of view, he had been given permission by Samuel's partner, Kiraz—permission he tried to confirm in a letter to Kiraz on October 1.

Two days later the Hebrew Daily, *Davar*, carried an article, headlined "DISCOVERY LAST YEAR OF GENIZAH [repository for worn-out Jewish scrolls] FROM JUDAEAN WILDERNESS," informing the Israeli public for the first time in detail about the discovery of the first Dead Sea Scrolls.

It was not long before various scholars also began to comb ancient literature for references which might illuminate this discovery. At least three references to scrolls previously discovered in the vicinity of Jericho were found: one in the early third century, one in the early 9th century, and another in the 10th century.

Again, in November 1948, George Isha'ya, Kando, and others excavated Cave 1 (or, one of the caves) and secured more fragments. At about the same time the April copies of the *Bulletin of the American Schools of Oriental Research* (*BASOR*) reached Jerusalem. Imagine their surprise when G. W. L. Harding, Chief Curator (later, Director) of the Antiquities Department of Jordan, and Fr. Roland de Vaux, President of the Board of Trustees of the

Palestine Archaeological Museum, learned about this important discovery for the very

Khirbet Qumran before full excavation. © John C. Trever

first time. Harding was livid, and de Vaux wasn't much calmer. They should have been informed months before by the scholars who had been working with the scrolls, and now they were the "last to know."

Even worse, although Harding and de Vaux did not yet know this, Samuel had long since decided to take the scrolls to the United States. He had more or less said that to Sukenik, through Kiraz, in his February letter. Toward the end of 1948 Samuel's chance came unexpectedly when the Patriarch appointed him "Apostolic Delegate to the United States and Canada." With everyone distracted by the war, Samuel made his way to Beirut,

De Vaux excavating at Murabba'at. Courtesy of the École Biblique et Archéologique Française de Jérusalem

Wadi Murabba'at. Courtesy of the Israel Antiquities Authority

where he collected the scrolls from storage and boarded the *S. S. Excalibur* in Beirut for a journey that was to take him through many ports and last three weeks. When he landed in Jersey City, New Jersey on January 29, 1949, he was met by a delegation of Syrian Christians. The Dead Sea Scrolls had reached the United States, hidden in the Metropolitan's luggage.

The Search Continues: 1949

From 1949 onward, the center of scrolls acquisition became the privately owned Palestine Archaeological Museum (PAM) in East Jerusalem (Jordan), and the central players, Harding, de Vaux, and the PAM's secretary, Yusef Saad. It was not to be long before Harding and de Vaux had to face the reality of illegal excavation square in the face. To their great credit, they were to make a momentous, fortuitous decision about how to handle the Bedouin, antiquities dealers, and their booty.

But by January 1949 none of the officials of the Palestine Archaeological Museum or the Department of Antiquities even knew the precise location of Cave 1. This was the obvious starting point if any control at all were to be brought to the Bedouin treasure hunting. The Department appealed to Captain Philippe Lippens, Belgian observer on the United Nations staff, who in turn asked for help from Major-General Lash of the Arab Legion to relocate the cave. This was accomplished on 28 January 1949 by Captain Akkash Basha al-Zebn after several days of searching.

A serious controversy arose over the lack of notification of the proper authorities on the part of the Bedouin and Kando, but especially Sukenik, Trever, Brownlee, and Burrows, and continued for some months. When all was said and done, the only conclusion one could draw was that none of the principles involved had kept the letter of the law. Harding, increasingly angry, was on the verge of prosecuting those he could. Eventually, however, Harding and de Vaux realized that scrolls discovered later would never be recovered through normal channels, and they, together with Saad, gradually came up with a system of accommodation to the facts on the ground. They entered into an agreement with Kando stipulating that if he would first offer to the PAM the scrolls coming onto the antiquities market, neither he nor his sources, usually Bedouin, would be prosecuted. For now, Harding and de Vaux realized, the most important thing was to excavate the cave and find whatever might have been missed by the Bedouin and their compatriots during multiple visits over the past two years.

After they had "re-discovered" Cave 1, it took Harding and de Vaux just two weeks to organize the official excavation. Under their direction the joint effort of the École Biblique, the American Schools of Oriental Research (ASOR), the Department of Antiquities of Jordan (DAJ), and the Museum (PAM), lasted three weeks during February-March 1949.

Two weeks after the completion of this excavation, Harding, as "Chief Curator of Antiquities" [of Jordan], composed a "Communiqué to the Press" (March 21, 1949).

Cave 4 Team member, Józef Milik, with a large stash of pottery bowls discovered at Qumran. Courtesy of the Israel Antiquities Authority

In this communiqué he recounts the main points he had made or was to make elsewhere about the scrolls: *It is deeply to be regretted that those who received the earliest information about the find in 1947 and 1948 did not take all possible steps to ensure the proper handling and treatment of the original excavation of the cave.*

At almost the same time de Vaux and Harding were excavating Cave 1 at Qumran, Mar Samuel, now on the other side of

De Vaux examining sherds at Qumran. Courtesy of *École Biblique et Archéologique Française de Jérusalem*

the Atlantic and undeterred by a mysterious, anonymous attempt to derail his efforts to sell the scrolls, learned the "lay of the land" with astonishing speed. Only weeks after arriving in the States, he met with Albright at Johns Hopkins University in March 1949. Albright advised him that the value of the scrolls could not possibly be less than $180,000. Below that price, Albright said, "no intelligent man versed in books would dare to go." One can only imagine how this large sum turned Samuel's head!

Back in the new state of Jordan, the "Harding-de Vaux Plan" bore almost immediate fruit. During the spring of 1950, Saad succeeded in purchasing further Cave 1 fragments for £1,000 from Kando in Bethlehem: 6 fragments of Isaiah[b], 8 fragments of the Genesis Apocryphon, and fragments of the Annex to the Rule of the Community. Without fully realizing what they had done, Harding and de Vaux had put in place an apparatus for saving the scrolls that remained for decades; and it was soon tested—sorely so.

New Discoveries: Murabba'at, 1951

The first hint of a new discovery came in October 1951. Without warning, several Ta'amireh Bedouin boldly presented themselves at the Palestine Archaeological Museum in Jerusalem. In their hands were two fragments of skin on which were inscribed Hebrew and Greek letters. The Bedouin would give no information about the source of these new scrolls, so Harding and de Vaux did only what they could: they took the matter under advisement.

Having already planned to excavate at Qumran beginning toward the end of November 1951, Harding and de Vaux saw no reason to change their plans. They had no idea where the new scrolls cache was, nor any easy way to find out. But events began to unfold fast. At the very moment de Vaux and Harding were excavating at Qumran, Kando and George brought more fragments to the École Biblique in Jerusalem. Naturally, they claimed they were from Qumran Cave 1, but the appearance of these new scroll fragments was so different de Vaux knew immediately that they came from another location. After considerable investigation, negotiation, and even a little subterfuge, de Vaux and Harding located the new scrolls site: the now very famous Wadi Murabba'at.

Harding and de Vaux dropped everything at Qumran immediately and headed south to Murabba'at, about halfway to Ein Gedi, to mount a full-fledged excavation of the rather remote and inaccessible four caves, already plundered by Bedouin. Later, a fifth cave would be found in the area during March 1955.

De Vaux and Harding found "large quantities of cloth, basket work, ropes, etc., as well as parchment and papyrus scroll fragments inscribed in Greek, Hebrew and Aramaic." Most of the documents were from the early second century CE, among them a Greek marriage contract from the 7th year of the Roman Emperor Hadrian, 124 CE, fragments from biblical books, and personal documents *in Hebrew* from "Simeon ben Kosibah, Prince of Israel" (Simeon bar Kokhba).

This was especially significant since most scholars had previously concluded that Aramaic so completely overcame Hebrew during the Second Temple period that Hebrew simply ceased to be a common spoken and written colloquial language. Such Hebrew documents, and other later discoveries among the Dead Sea Scrolls were to force the next generation of scholars to reconsider the linguistic variety of Palestine in the centuries just before, during, and after Jesus' lifetime.

The bulk of the Murabba'at material was bought up rather quickly. In at least sixteen separate transactions with at least eleven different people between December 22, 1951 and August 26, 1952, Murabba'at fragments, as well as some pottery and other objects, came to the Palestine Archaeological Museum, for which it expended US$6,685. Only a few items from Murabba'at straggled in much later, the last recorded purchase of Murabba'at fragments being in 1958.

Caves 2 and 3, Qumran, 1952

The second cave at Qumran was discovered near the first in February 1952. De Vaux returned to Qumran from Murabba'at during March 1952. Having decided that a systematic survey of the surrounding area was long overdue, especially in light of the recent Bedouin discovery and illegal excavation of caves at Murabba'at, de Vaux and William Reed, Director of the American School in Jerusalem, set out to explore caves in the Qumran region.

In order to cover an area about four kilometers in both directions, north and south, along the high, rugged cliffs overlooking the western shore of the Dead Sea, they divided their colleagues and Bedouin workers into three teams: one led by Fr. Dominique Barthélemy, another by Fr. Józef Milik, and a third led by Henri de Contenson. They remained camped at Qumran, but left each morning on their survey, and returned each evening at dusk.

Of the 225 caves the teams eventually surveyed, 37 were further investigated, and 25 were found to contain sherds of pottery similar to those discovered at Qumran, as well as remnants of cloth similar to the scroll wrappings found in Cave 1.

Late one afternoon, as de Contenson's party was returning to the encampment at Qumran for the night, one of the Bedouin noticed a potsherd, a pottery fragment of obvious antiquity, lying on the ground near a small cave opening. Still about four kilometers north of Qumran, with darkness approaching swiftly, Henri de Contenson realized there was nothing they could do at the moment, but they marked the spot with a stick and returned the following day.

Although this cave hardly looked promising, more like a pile of rocks because most of the roof had collapsed, de Contenson and his team broke through the rocks blocking the opening, and entered what was left of the cave. On the last day of working, just as they were finishing up, de Contenson and Milik found what was to become known as the Copper Scroll, the only metal Dead Sea Scroll, containing a list of hidden treasures.

Area with caves near Qumran. James Davis; Eye Ubiquitous/Corbis

Perspective of Qumran and the Dead Sea taken from the high cliffs, looking east, with the "Hills of Moab" (Jordan) in the distance. © John C. Trever

Khirbet Mird, 1952

By July 1952 the Ta'amireh tribe's constant clandestine examination of the area had borne fruit again. They discovered another cache of manuscripts near the ruins of a Christian monastery at Khirbet Mird, about five miles from Qumran: fragments in Early Arabic, Syriac, and some New Testament Greek, all dating to the Byzantine Period, approximately 6th-7th centuries CE. About six months later, the site was excavated by R. de Langhe of the University of Louvain, and most of the fragments were taken to Belgium, where they still remain.

Nahal Hever, 1952

During July and August, 1952, Bedouin brought manuscripts to Jerusalem, including a Greek text of the Minor Prophets, from an "unidentified" cave, probably Nahal Hever (Wadi Khabra). Then, as summer waned, de Vaux and Harding began to get clues about an even greater discovery. This time, it did not take the Bedouin long to start bringing the new finds to the attention of the Palestine Archaeological Museum

The two pieces of the Copper Scroll as they were found in Qumran Cave 3. Courtesy of the Israel Antiquities Authority

and Harding. By now, after having worked so closely with so many from the Ta'amireh tribe, Harding and de Vaux were considered friends, and both the trust and the arrangements necessary for buying and selling were firmly in place.

Qumran Cave 4, 1952

The first fragments from a new cave at Qumran arrived in Jerusalem on September 20, 1952 (or possibly as much as two weeks earlier, since there is some confusion in the written records). Within two days, over the weekend, de Vaux and Harding put together a team and excavated this fourth cave during the last week of the month. Oddly, they had overlooked this cave, in close proximity to the Qumran site, during their search campaign earlier that year.

Although the Bedouin had already stripped the cave of many of its fragments the archaeologists discovered a small underground chamber the Bedouins had not reached. In this cave (actually two caves) archaeologists found fragments belonging to about 100 different manuscripts, almost all represented among the fragments bought from the Bedouin, confirming the origin of the batches the Bedouin had sold in Jerusalem some days before.

It was immediately apparent to de Vaux and Harding that they had a serious problem. The amount of money necessary to rescue the vast collection of Cave 4 fragments threatened to overwhelm the financial resources of the privately endowed Palestine Archaeological Museum.

De Vaux later reported:

> While Cave 4 was being emptied,

Location of several caves, looking north from Qumran. © John C. Trever

the surrounding area was being explored as well. Very near Cave 4, Cave 5 was found containing the remains of about fifteen manuscripts. The small Cave 6, from which the Bedouin had only shortly before removed a certain number of fragments belonging to more than twenty manuscripts, was located. The two batches presented on September 20 and

Qumran Cave 4A. The far entrance leads to 4B. © Diane Fields

the finds harvested during the official excavation, however, only represented the lesser part of the discovery: many of the fragments were still in the hands of the Bedouins. Taking the advice of G. L. Harding, Director of Antiquities, and aware of the importance of the glorious discovery for the country, the Jordanian Government allocated a sum of JD 15,000 (US $42,000) to buy the two batches, which already had been stored in a safe place, and which could be acquired. Given the limits of its budget and the urgent, and sometimes tragic, requirements its funds had to satisfy, this enlightened generosity on the part of the Jordanian Government deserves the recognition of the scholarly world.

More Cave 4 fragments; Sukenik dies, 1953

The pace of scrolls acquisition continued to accelerate in 1953. Cave 4 fragments were still in the hands of the Bedouin and Kando. Eventually it was agreed that foreign institutions contributing funds for the purchase of fragments would receive an allotment of fragments once scholars finished preparing them for publication. Harding began to put together a team of eight scholars (the "Cave 4 Team") to sort, identify, reconstruct, and decipher this vast hoard in preparation for publication.

Meanwhile, on the other side of divided Jerusalem, Israelis were almost completely unaware of the new discoveries. Sukenik passed away without seeing the publication of the scrolls he had bought for Hebrew University, disappointed, but not as disappointed as he would have been had he known how many more scrolls were just beyond his reach only a few streets away!

The St. Mark's Scrolls return to Jerusalem, 1954

Then, on June 1, 1954 Yigael Yadin, Sukenik's son, received an unexpected call from New York. He was informed that the St. Mark's Scrolls were being advertised for sale by Mar Samuel in the *Wall Street Journal*. By June 11, 1954 an agreement was reached between Samuel and a "Mr. Green" (a pseudonym adopted by Prof. Harry Orlinsky of the Jewish Institute of Religion) to purchase the scrolls for $250,000. The sale was finalized on July 1. Mar Samuel only later learned that he had been tricked into selling the scrolls to Israel, or at least he claimed to have been tricked. After he left the Waldorf-Astoria Hotel, where the exchange had taken place, Yadin and his colleagues noticed that a piece of the Habakkuk Commentary was missing. They called Mar Samuel in New Jersey, who checked among his miscellaneous remaining fragments and found the piece. Samuel *mailed* it to the Waldorf the next day! On February 13, 1955 Yadin announced publicly the return of the St. Mark's scrolls to Jerusalem, to be joined with those purchased by his father in 1947.

Qumran Caves 7-10; Masada, 1955

Back in Jordan, Caves 7, 8, 9, and 10 were discovered in the terraces surrounding Qumran during de Vaux's fourth season of excavation in the spring of 1955. These yielded only small amounts of scroll fragments, but that same spring a Hebrew scroll of the Minor Prophets was discovered by Bedouin in Murabba'at Cave 5. Farther down the coast of the Dead Sea in Israeli territory an expedition to Masada directed by Yadin discovered one papyrus document, foreshadowing other manuscript finds there in years to come.

Qumran Cave 11; the Suez Crisis, 1956

Bedouin discovered the eleventh and final scroll cave in the Qumran area in February 1956, but acquisition of the new scrolls was difficult. As usual, there were no funds, but even worse, political tensions in the Middle East were high yet again. This time a confrontation between Britain and France on one side, and Egypt and the Arab world on the other, had developed over, among other things, the ownership and administration of the Suez Canal. By June anti-British feeling in Jordan had reached fever pitch. Virtually every British employee of the government was dismissed. In one of the most unfortunate incidents in the whole story of the scrolls, Harding was forcibly removed from his position as Director-General of the Department of Antiquities of Jordan. Although he retained his position with the still private Palestine Archaeological Museum, he took

up residence in Harissa, near Beirut, Lebanon. This was a blow to the acquisition and publication of the scrolls from which the project never fully recovered.

On July 26, 1956 Egyptian President Nasser nationalized the Suez Canal and all of its assets. Owing to the ensuing Suez Crisis/Sinai War that autumn, the Cave 4

Prof. Yigael Yadin with one of the scrolls and two scroll jars.

Team's restoration and deciphering of the scrolls was completely halted. All the Dead Sea Scrolls in the Palestine Archaeological Museum were removed to the vault of the Ottoman Bank in Amman for safekeeping. They were not returned to Jerusalem for six months (March 1957).

Further Discoveries, 1958-1965

The Bedouin never stopped searching. During the spring of 1958 they discovered

G.W.L. Harding, Director of the Department of Antiquities of Jordan (left), inside Cave 4 at Qumran in late 1952 or early 1953. Hulton Archive/Getty Images

scroll fragments in a cave near En Gedi, farther south along the Dead Sea from Qumran in Israeli territory, and brought them to the attention of archaeologists.

On the Jordanian side the Palestine Archaeological Museum had exhausted its resources. Nevertheless, a second gift from McCormick Theological Seminary (Chicago) and a gift from the All Soul's Unitarian Church in New York made it possible to purchase the last of the Cave 4 scroll fragments (or at least the last of those Kando admitted to having at the time).

During March 1959 Israeli archaeologists returned to Nahal Hever, unearthing about forty papyrus business documents in Hebrew, Aramaic, Nabataean, and Greek dating from about 88 CE to 132 CE. Early the following year rumors of fragments brought to Jerusalem by Bedouin from Nahal Se'elim resulted in a survey of the valley by Israeli archaeologist Yohanan Aharoni, but documentary fragments were found only in one cave. The same year (1960) Yadin excavated the "Cave of Letters" (Cave 5/6) in Nahal Hever, discovering the immensely important "Bar Kokhba letters" as well as fragments of Psalms and 15 letters in Hebrew, Aramaic, and Greek.

Back in the United States, Prof. Frank Cross, a member of the Cave 4 Team assigned to reconstruct, decipher, and publish the materials from that cave, continued to look for funds to buy the Cave 11 scrolls,

lying in the Palestine Archaeological Museum's vault unopened and unread, awaiting

Prof. Yigael Yadin standing in front of the Cave of the Letters. Hulton Archive/Getty Images.

"redemption," since 1956. Cross negotiated, on behalf of American Schools of Oriental Research, the purchase of "research and publication rights" to the Cave 11 Psalms Scroll from Kando for $60,000, donated by Elizabeth Bechtel, but according to the

49

Cave 4A, showing one of the now much-eroded top entrances. © Diane Fields

agreement between the Museum and Kando, none of the other Cave 11 scrolls could even be examined until they were paid for. After the transaction was complete, the Psalms Scroll was assigned to Prof. James A. Sanders for publication.

Shortly afterward the Dutch Royal Academy, in two separate transactions, agreed with the Palestine Archaeological Museum to purchase publication rights for the Targum of Job and other Cave 11 Aramaic and Hebrew fragments. Two Dutch scholars, Fr. Van der Ploeg (who had seen the Great Isaiah Scroll in Jerusalem in 1947) and Prof. A. Van der Woude were among those assigned to the task. They published their scrolls quite quickly with the famous publishing house in Leiden, E. J. Brill.

Unfortunately, from time to time, fragments disappeared or were stolen from the PAM. The worst incident occurred in April 1960. Five fragments were stolen from the scrollery: one of Deuteronomy, a large one of Samuel, and three of Daniel. These have never been recovered, and must still be in a private collection somewhere. A few other incidents of disappearing or stolen scrolls are even more mysterious.

From March 14-27, 1961 Yadin

mounted a second expedition to Nahal Hever and discovered the "Babata Archive," and land contracts originally from En Gedi. During this period also Aharoni excavated the "Cave of Horrors."

From the left in the foreground, Yadin and De Vaux together at Masada. Courtesy of Alain Chambon, École Biblique et Archéologique Française de Jérusalem

Then on August 5, 1961, after years of threats and unsuccessful attempts, the Hashemite Kingdom of Jordan revoked all past agreements concerning eventual transfer of scrolls to donors who provided funds for their purchase from the Bedouin. The government "nationalized" the scrolls, seizing ownership from the Palestine Archaeological Museum, where, however, they continued to be housed.

Meanwhile, the Bedouin were far from finished. In 1962 they discovered about forty papyrus documents (known as the Samaria papyri), dating to the 4th century BCE, in a large cave in Wadi ed-Daliyeh, about nine miles north of Jericho. Late that year Cross arrived in Jerusalem on behalf of ASOR with $20,000 to buy these papyri, but by the time the whole typically Middle Eastern saga of intrigue and deception was finished, the final price was $30,000.

During the next three years excavators working under Yadin at Masada discovered fragments of many manuscripts, including Hebrew, Greek, and Latin documents. Three especially important fragmentary papyrus manuscripts were among them: Psalms 81-85, Songs of the Sabbath Sacrifice (also found at Qumran), and five chapters of a first-century BCE scroll of Ben-Sirach (Ecclesiasticus).

All this time, some Cave 11 materials had continued to lie in the Palestine Archaeological Museum's vault. Cross began negotiating with Kando for the purchase of the 11 Qpaleo-Hebrew Leviticus scroll on behalf of ASOR, available for JD 8,000 (US $23,000); but the negotiation was suspended when the museum was nationalized by the government of Jordan on August 6, 1966.

Early in 1967 Cross was approached about Cave 11 material that had apparently never been offered for sale to the PAM and was still in Kando's possession. That spring Cross flew to Israel, crossed the border, and drove to Beirut to negotiate for these scrolls. In a nocturnal clandestine meeting under a bridge outside the city, Kando showed him several boxes of fragments, some from Cave 11, others from the Bar Kokhba era. Kando also offered a "large scroll," later known as the "Temple Scroll," or the "White Scroll," but did not have it with him and no agreement was reached. Highly disappointed, Cross returned to the States empty handed. Some of these fragments have never been seen by scholars again.

The "Six-Day War" broke out on June 4, 1967. Dr. Awni Dajani, reportedly the first Arab Ph.D. in Archaeology, Director-General of the Department of Antiquities of Jordan, had set out from Amman, having taken upon himself the responsibility of transporting the scrolls from Jerusalem, but was forced to turn back because the Amman-Jerusalem road had been severely cratered by bombing. When Israeli troops captured the Palestine Archaeological Museum after a fierce gun battle, they found all the Dead Sea Scrolls packed in wooden crates in the basement, ready for transfer to Jordan, but still in Jerusalem, where they remain to this day. With war still raging, the moment Israel captured Bethlehem Yadin sent soldiers to Kando's home. They forced him to hand over the Temple Scroll, hidden there for more than ten years. Kando was eventually paid $110,000 for this scroll, only a small portion of what it was worth at the time.

Over the years since 1967 there have been several further discoveries of scroll

Inside Cave 4 at Qumran, June 1, 1956. © James Whitmore, Time Life Pictures/Getty Images

fragments, showing that just as archaeolo-gists suspected, not everything was discov-ered in the 1950s and 1960s. It has become increasingly clear, too, that not everything found during those early years was brought to the proper authorities. A few scrolls—no one knows how many for sure—still remain in the hands of collectors and dealers

וחתות שדמו שדם וחמס ארץ קריה וכל יושבי בה

פשר הדבר על הכוהן הרשע לשלם לו את

גמולו אשר גמל על אביונים כיא הלבנון הוא

עצת היחד והבהמות המה פתאי יהודה עושה

התורה אשר ישופטנו אל לכלה

כאשר זמם לכלות אביונים ואשר אמר מדמי

קריה וחמס ארץ פשרו הקריה היא ירושלם

אשר פעל בה הכוהן מעשי תועבות ויטמא את

מקדש אל וחמס ארץ המה ערי יהודה אשר

גזל הון אביונים הוי הבוצע בצע רע לביתו

כמה בה ימרו שקר כיא בטח יער וצריו עליון

לעשות אלולים אלמם פשר הדבר על נול

כיא אבני הגבית אשר יצרום לעובדים ולשתחות

להמה והבת לוא יצילום ביום ה... עפ אין

The Habakkuk Commentary (1QpHab), column 12.

1 will appall you, owing to the human blood and the violence (done to) the country, the city and all who dwell there.

2 The interpretation of the word concerns the Wicked Priest, to pay him the

3 reward for what he did to the poor. Because Lebanon is

4 the Council of the Community and the animals are the simple folk of Judah, those who observe

5 the Law. God will sentence him to destruction, Blank

6 exactly as he intended to destroy the poor. And as for what he says: Hab 2:17 "Owing to the blood

7 of the city and the violence (done to) the country". Its interpretation: the city is Jerusalem

8 in which the /Wicked/ Priest performed repulsive acts and defiled

9 the Sanctuary of God. The violence (done to) the country are the cities of Judah which

10 he plundered of the possessions of the poor. Hab 2:18 What use is the sculpture which the craftsman carves,

11 (or) the cast effigy and sham oracle, in whom their craftsman trusts,

12 to make dumb idols? The interpretation of the word concerns all the

13 idols of the peoples which they made, to serve them and bow down

14 for them. But they will not save them on the day of Judgment. Hab 2:19-20 Woe,

15 wo[e, to anyone saying] to wood: Wake up! and to a silent [st]one: G[et up!]

16 [Can it instruct? It is covered with gold and silver, but no]

17 [spirit at all is therein. But YHWH is in his holy Temple.]

(*The Dead Sea Scrolls Study Edition*, Vol. 1, ed. and transl. by F. García Martínez and E.J.C. Tigchelaar [Leiden: Brill, 1997])

The west coast of the Dead Sea south of Qumran. Carl and Ann Purcell/Corbis

Chapter 2

STUDY AND PUBLICATION

Prof. Yigael Yadin preparing his edition of the Temple Scroll in his study in Jerusalem, May 1968. © Ted Spiegel/Corbis

Publication of the Dead Sea Scrolls went in three different directions from the beginning, mainly because by 1950 there were three separate collections. In the new State of Israel Sukenik had at his disposal three scrolls in addition to a few fragments: Isaiah^b, the Thanksgiving Scroll (*Hodayot*) and the War Scroll. He began to prepare a publication that included photographs, transcriptions, and lists of textual variants. A preliminary report appeared in 1948, a Hebrew edition was issued in 1950, and the complete edition was published in Hebrew and English by the Hebrew University, posthumously, in 1955.

Meanwhile, in the United States Trever, Brownlee, and Burrows had photographs of three scrolls in hand, with permission from Mar Samuel to publish them: Isaiah^a, the Habakkuk Commentary and the Manual of Discipline. They published photographs only of the first two in 1950 and the latter in 1951, without transcriptions or textual commentary. The extremely brittle Genesis Apocryphon was not yet unrolled.

The situation in Jordan was very different. The third group of scrolls available in 1950 consisted of fragments from Cave 1 discovered by the official excavation in 1949 and those purchased by Saad from Kando in 1950. Harding and de Vaux envisioned something much more elaborate

Gerald W. Lankester Harding, Director of the Department of Antiquities of Jordan, examining scroll fragments in 1953. Hulton-Deutsch/Corbis

for their publication. Offers were solicited from three different publishers. Harding chose Oxford University Press with whom he concluded a contract on behalf

The École Biblique et Archéologique Française and Monastery of St. Stephen, Jerusalem. Courtesy École Biblique et Archéologique Française de Jérusalem

of the Palestine Archaeological Museum. De Vaux assigned two young scholars then at the École Biblique in Jerusalem, Frs. Barthélemy and Milik, to edit the texts. Both exceedingly gifted, they worked fast and efficiently, setting the standards for future volumes. By 1953 they had submitted their manuscript to Oxford University Press. In those days, when every book was set in "hot type," and the fastest communication between Jordan and England was airmail, it was considered reasonable that the first volume of *Discoveries in the Judae-*

an Desert (DJD) appeared two years later, toward the end of 1955.

In the meantime the entire world of scrolls had been turned upside down. While Barthélemy and Milik were editing those Cave 1 fragments the discovery and purchase of the vast new hoards at Wadi Murabba'at and Caves 1-6, particularly Cave 4, completely overwhelmed the financial resources of the Palestine Archaeological Museum. But there was an even bigger problem: what would be done with the thousands of fragments now that the Museum had them? Then in the spring of 1953, just as Barthélemy and Milik were finishing up the first volume of DJD, Barthélemy became severely ill and returned to France.

That left Milik as the only experienced scrolls scholar in Jordan. In order to bring some order to the situation considerably more manpower was called for. Harding and de Vaux decided a larger team of scholars should be appointed to work specifically on the thousands of Cave 4 fragments coming into their possession. At that point, however, no one had any idea how many more fragments yet remained in the hands of the Bedouin and Kando, nor did they know that it would take another five years, until 1958, to bring the last of them into the Museum, or at least the last of them Kando was willing to part with at the time.

In his capacity as Curator of the Museum Harding took charge of the appointment of the Cave 4 Team. The team was to be composed of two representatives from each of the four prominent schools of archaeology represented on the Museum's Board: French, American, British and German. The political situation made it impossible to include representation from Israel. Harding contacted each of the four schools. The École Biblique put forward Milik. Had Barthélemy not fallen ill or had he recovered in time, he would have been the second, but his recovery was slow and he never returned

Part of the Cave 4 Team outside the Palestine Archaeological Museum. Courtesy of the Israel Antiquities Authority

to Jerusalem as a resident again. His place was taken by a specialist in Aramaic dialects, Fr. Jean Starcky.

The American School's first member was Frank Moore Cross, a young scholar who began his work in the spring of 1953. The second member was a more seasoned scholar from the Catholic University of America, Fr. Patrick Skehan, who arrived in Jerusalem in 1954.

The British contingent was not as easily filled out. Harding asked G. Driver at Ox-

ford for recommendations. His first two, P. Wernberg-Møller and J. A. Emerton were invited but could not accept. His third, John Strugnell, and fourth, John Allegro, both joined the team in 1954.

The German School only came up with one name, Claus-Hunno Hunziger, who arrived in Jerusalem in 1954. With his appointment the team numbered seven, brought to eight a few years later with the addition of a third member from the French School, Fr. Maurice Baillet.

Subsequently, two terms came to be applied to this team that were never mentioned in the early years at all: "international" and "inter-confessional." The team was international to be sure, but only because it reflected the constituency of the Museum's Board of Trustees. It was inter-confessional only by accident: three Catholics, three Protestants and a former Protestant, now lapsed. Religious affiliation had nothing at all to do with the original appointments. Only in the wake of later criticism, largely instigated by Allegro, that Catholics had somehow monopolized the scrolls or conspired to hide passages potentially embarrassing or damaging to Christianity, was the team called "inter-confessional."

To the several hats he already wore, Fr.

de Vaux now added another. He was already Prior of the Dominican Monastery of St. Stephen, which hosted the École Biblique et Archéologique Française de Jérusalem of which he was also the Director. In addition he was the director of the archaeological excavation

constructed, identification of biblical and other texts already known were made, and even more exhilarating, a whole new world of previously unknown Jewish literature emerged from the past.

Although Harding said nothing about future publication in his invitations to the Cave 4 Team, everyone assumed that this would be the end result of the cleaning, sorting, reconstruction, transcription, deciphering, and translation comprising the work of those first months and years. But at this early stage there was no overarching publication plan, there was no financial plan, there wasn't even any precise conception of how many volumes it might take to publish the vast hoard. For Harding and de Vaux the whole thing was a moving target. Eventually, they came up with an estimate of four volumes.

2-3 The "Scrollery" inside the Palestine Archaeological Museum. In the foreground on the left, Msgr. Patrick Skehan, Cave 4 Team member. Courtesy of the Israel Antiquities Authority

of Cave 1 and then the excavation of Khirbet Qumran, as well as the President of the Board of Trustees of the Palestine Archaeological Museum. In addition to all these responsibilities he became director of the Cave 4 Team.

This team of five junior and two senior scholars was off to a roaring start. Excitement was high, new discoveries in the scrolls and new identifications of fragments were an almost daily occurrence. Fragments were fitted together, documents were re-

Through all this process de Vaux seems to have been a rather benign overseer who allowed the Team to organize itself. Little by little groups of manuscripts emerged: biblical texts in Hebrew, biblical texts in Paleo-Hebrew script, non-biblical Hebrew texts, non-biblical Aramaic texts, etc. A system evolved by which "lots" or groups of manuscripts were collected on the basis of content, language, script or a combination of these, and "assigned" to each team member by consensus. Those "assignments," casual at first, became more and more concrete until some years down the road they came to be jealously guarded possessions. While one can very well understand the proprietary feeling attached to documents one has reconstructed, and in some cases discovered or helped to purchase, in hindsight this development was, perhaps not entirely felicitous.

In the various archives of letters surviving from those first two years there is evidence of a great camaraderie among the members of the Team, but toward the end of 1955 one begins to see that there is trouble in paradise, a "fly in the ointment." Young Allegro became persuaded that he saw elements in the scrolls that would call into question the very foundations of Christianity. He did not hide his glee. Like many formerly enthusiastic religious adherents who feel they were duped, who feel they have "seen the light" and have rejected their former beliefs, he was now ardently against what he had once believed. Allegro had become not just passively agnostic or atheist, but stridently so.

Father Rolland de Vaux. Courtesy École Biblique et Archéologique Française de Jérusalem

His fellow team members did not share his views about the scrolls and challenged him to substantiate them. He publicized his views both in print and on the air, making what the other Team members contended were unfounded, even dishonest, claims. In an open letter to the *Times* of London several team members distanced themselves from him and his views. But Allegro would not retract: the gauntlet had been thrown down. Accusations, increasingly nasty, flew back and forth by airmail. Allegro whipped both himself and the public into a frenzy of suspicion about conspiracies of silence and deception. The developing rift between Allegro and the Cave 4 Team grew deeper, and despite several attempts at reconciliation, was never bridged. Allegro's impatience over the publication of the Copper Scroll only made it worse.

Meanwhile the remainder of the Team avoided publicity and controversy. They worked hard and they were productive, especially Milik and Strugnell, whose personal situations enabled them to live in Jerusalem nearly full-time.

The work was extremely taxing. Few

scholars could have kept up the pace. Indeed, a few hours trying to put these pieces together into coherent documents, trying to fill in the blanks, trying to make sense out of a handwriting that often has to be read with

John Strugnell piecing together Cave 4 scroll fragments in 1958. Courtesy of the Israel Antiquities Authority

a magnifying glass or a microscope, would be enough to convince most people that their talents lie elsewhere.

More than the difficulty of the work itself, many other factors hindered or slowed them down during those early years, and it seemed new ones kept popping up. There were also the normal vicissitudes of life that most of us share: financial worries, family responsibilities, personal and spousal illnesses and professional demands.

And time after time political events con-spired against them too. As we have said, the scrolls were carted off to Amman during the Suez crisis, making them inaccessible to the Team for half a year during 1956–1957. When they returned to Jerusalem some scrolls were damaged by mold. The German teammember, Claus-Hunno Hunzinger spent much of the summer of 1957 cleaning them. Harding's dis-missal from the Department of Antiquities of Jordan, fur-thermore, crippled the entire operation, for it was Harding who had appointed the Team, signed the contracts with Ox-ford, dealt most directly with donors, and brought to the enterprise wisdom and or-ganizational skills that were never replaced.

The financial structure for publication was likewise problematic. Well into the 1960s it continued to be dif-ficult to find funding for purchasing, much less publishing, the scrolls. Some funding to assist the Cave 4 Team came from the Rock-efeller family, but this was discontinued by 1960. The scrolls were nationalized by Jor-dan in 1961 resulting in broken promises to donors–not exactly a fundraiser's dream. The Museum did not take full advantage of the fundraising possibilities of exhibitions. When a donation was received, the imme-diate needs were so great that nothing was saved back to help secure the next donation.

There was no foreign tax-exempt apparatus for channeling funds directly to the Museum. Of all the factors retarding the publication, lack of funding was among the most prominent at that stage. Still, Volume 2 of DJD, the Wadi Murabba'at scrolls, appeared in 1961, and the Cave 3 materials in 1962 (the texts in both mostly prepared by Milik) and the Cave 11 Psalms Scroll, edited by J. A. Sanders, came out in 1965.

As if all the other difficulties were not enough, Jordan nationalized the Museum in 1966 and war broke out in 1967, uniting Jerusalem under Israeli control. Although the Israeli government left de Vaux in charge of Discoveries in the Judaean Desert and the Cave 4 Team, it took over the Palestine Archaeological Museum itself, including all the scrolls housed there from Qumran Caves 1–11, Murabba'at, and other Judean Desert sites under Jordanian control since 1948. The Museum was renamed after its original benefactor, John D. Rockefeller, Jr. Over the course of time scholars were reduced to working in a tiny basement room, a far cry from the spacious quarters they had previously enjoyed.

The project was essentially in limbo for several years after 1967. Gradually, over a period of years, Israel, first through its Department of Antiquities and Museums, later reorganized as the Antiquities Authority, assumed responsibility for the safe-keeping, publication and conservation of these scrolls, but that did not happen all at once.

Then de Vaux died suddenly in 1971. Fr. Pierre Benoit, also from the École, assumed his mantle in 1972. Fr. Benoit has been criticized for not being as vigorous or demanding as one might have wished. To be fair, however, publication continued to advance during the thirteen years of his leadership, which he

Prof. John Strugnell, Cave 4 team member and Editor in Chief 1985-1990 in front of the École Biblique et Archéologique Française de Jérusalem, July 1, 1990. Time Life Pictures/Getty Images

continued to provide until 1985, two years before his death in 1987 at the age of 81.

Through all these years Milik continued to be the most productive in terms of actual publication, a great wonder considering his own tragedies and traumas–bouts of severe manic-depression, other physical ailments and personal struggles, and a first marriage in his mid-forties for which he left the priest-hood. But intellectually he was a giant, an incredible linguist with a phenomenal memory and a skill for reading and identifying fragments unparalleled within the Cave 4 Team. When one surveys the extent of his scholarly articles, books, and contributions to *Discoveries in the Judaean Desert*, one cannot but be amazed. His *Ten Years of Discovery in the Wilderness of Judaea* alone was a major contribution, still immensely valuable nearly fifty years later.

Cross published important preliminary articles as well, and his very important *Ancient Library of Qumran and Modern Biblical Studies* continues to be used today in its third edition. Allegro was exceedingly prolific in the popular press. To his credit he was the first of the Cave 4 Team to publish his texts in Discoveries in the Judaean Desert (Vol. 5, 1968), but he was severely criticized for his shallow scholarship, and his volume is the only one of the series that is presently being revised.

It should be pointed out, however, that preliminary publications were a two-edged sword. They were beneficial because they put some information out in the public domain, gave opportunity for criticism, and resulted in improvements in the official publication.

But they consumed too much time, delayed final publication, and worst of all, tantalized to the point of distraction. The scholarly and public reaction was what one might expect from a starving man given just one bite off a full plate: initial gratitude turned to anger.

Through the 1970s and into the 1980s impatience with the seemingly slow pace of publication started to grow. By the late 1980s the outrage over the delayed publication of the Cave 4 scrolls was championed by the *Biblical Archaeology Review.* This delay and the inevitable conspiracy theories it engendered was the subject of several rather inaccurate books and articles in scholarly journals and even the popular press. Scrolls scholars were bombarded with criticism, most of it unfair and ill-informed. But it was there none the less.

The truth was that work had been ongoing. The Team had been slightly expanded, albeit somewhat belatedly. Cross and Strugnell supervised a large number of dissertations at Harvard dealing with the scrolls, many of which served as the basis for later publication, though they were not themselves as prolific, nor did they publish as quickly as some of their colleagues thought they should or could have. Quite unfairly, Strugnell, who gradually began taking over officially as editor in chief only in 1984-85 was blamed for all the "sins of the fathers." Many of his critics still do not realize he was editor in chief for only a little more than five years, and that in no small degree his years at the helm, during which only one volume appeared, bore fruit only on the next editor's watch. Nevertheless, by the summer of 1990 his personal and professional struggles had called into question his ability to continue to lead the publication team as editor in chief.

But conspiracies? Hardly. Mistakes, misfortunes, misadventures? Yes. In one sense the story of the publication of the scrolls has been a microcosm of life. It wasn't a perfect project and it wasn't run by perfect people. But the huge leap in publication that was to come from 1991 through 2001 was due not to outside criticism, not to pressure brought about from the illegal, unauthorized, unethical, unfair and premature publication on the part of some scholars and publishers. It came for other reasons and by other means entirely.

In the autumn of 1990 the newly convened Israel Antiquities Authority's Scrolls Oversight Committee asked Strugnell to step down, and appointed Prof. Emanuel Tov, formerly a student of Shemaryahu Talmon at Hebrew University and Strugnell and Cross at Harvard, as the new editor in chief. The continuing chief editor of biblical manuscripts was Prof. Eugene Ulrich of Notre Dame, also a student of Cross.

In November 1990, however, access to all the scrolls at the Rockefeller Museum was still severely limited, and many of the Cave 4 fragments were known to the general scholarly world only by name, if that. For a century it has been the scholarly norm that the publication of any antiquities was assigned to a scholar, and that scholar had the right of publication regardless of the time it took.

Certainly it would have been better had there been a greater expansion of the publication team in the 1970s and 1980s. The Cave 4 Team might have been more trusting of their colleagues to see the scrolls, or at least photographs, in order to know more about them, not to publish them. Yet, there were also good reasons for the Cave 4 Team to suspect that their years of work identifying fragments, creating documents out of small scraps and preparing them for publication would all be lost to poachers who would not respect their work nor give them credit. In the event that is exactly what did in some cases happen.

The growing impatience of scholars for unfettered and total access to the scrolls, the calls to "break the monopoly," to "disband the cartel," were epitomized by the release in the autumn of 1991 of an unauthorized publication of a more or less full set of photographs of most scrolls in the Rockefeller Museum in *A Facsimile Edition of the Dead Sea Scrolls: Prepared with an Introduction and Index by Robert H. Eisenman and James M. Robinson*, published by the *Biblical Archaeology Society*. The Israel Antiquities Authority contemplated legal action against those responsible for this volume, but decided against it.

By October 1991 matters had reached the breaking point and something had to be done. The final decision to make the scrolls accessible to the public was made by the Director of the Israel Antiquities Authority, Amir Drori, the Authority's Scrolls Oversight Committee, and the new editor in chief, Emanuel Tov. An edition of the Dead Sea Scrolls on microfiche, edited by Tov with

the collaboration of S. Pfann, was published in 1993 by Brill and IDC. The microfiches contained about 6,000 photographs of the scrolls from Qumran and other sites in the Judean Desert.

Nothing much changed after access to the scrolls was "opened." The fragments are extremely fragile. The care they had received over the years was not always optimal. It was obvious to anyone familiar with them that neither the general public nor even seasoned scholars would or should ever be allowed simply to examine them at will. But it was the *idea* of openness that was important. Under the new rules access was theoretically possible for anyone with good enough reasons and proper supervision. In fact few who had campaigned so tirelessly and acrimoniously for access ever actually bothered to apply for admission or to make the journey to Jerusalem, and even if they had, fewer still would have been able to read them. As for the photographs, they were already in the public domain, but few would know what they were seeing when they viewed them. Again, it was the idea, not the fact of openness that was the most important.

With the matter of access behind him, Tov moved forward quickly and vigorously. Naturally he stood on the shoulders of his predecessors: de Vaux, Benoit, and Strugnell; but he brought to the publication project a singleness of purpose, a talent for organization, an unswerving self-discipline, and a demanding leadership that had not previously been as evident as it might have. With the aid of the Oversight Committee he added many

members to the team, put in place a specialized group of assistants in Jerusalem for data entry, copy editing, and proofreading, made the most extensive use of personal computers and electronic communication possible in those days, persuaded Oxford University Press to publish volumes out of order as they were finished, reassigned texts where there was no hope that the original editors would ever finish them, and in general ran a very "tight ship." It paid off. And finally, there was enough money to do the job. With the financial and organizational backing of the Dead Sea Scrolls Foundation (through the generosity of a large number of individual donors), the Hebrew University of Jerusalem, and the Israel Antiquities Authority, together with money Strugnell had already secured from a donor in England and funds from the National Endowment for the Humanities for the team at Notre Dame, as well as support for at least one scholar by the Centre national de la recherche scientifique (CNRS, Paris), the project finally had a secure financial underpinning.

The publication team was eventually expanded to nearly 100 members from many countries, representing diverse branches of Christianity and Judaism, and in some cases, no religion at all. This national and religious diversity led to a long international cooperation on a level many organizations and countries can only dream about. What others have talked about, the Dead Sea Scrolls Publication Team has actually accomplished: an almost seamless interfaith, international working relationship with few difficulties based on differences of religion, race or nationality. The series, though not yet complete, is vast: *Discoveries in the Judaean Desert* now numbers 37 volumes. When combined with the volumes of the printed concordance (two so far) and materials such as those from Masada and elsewhere in the Judaean Desert, there will be more than 50 volumes of published Dead Sea Scrolls altogether.

At the same time the 1990s saw many other developments connected with the scrolls. There was a spate of new books and the emergence of the Internet made a whole host of websites possible. The microfiche edition gave wide access to the photographs, and both a set of CD-ROM photographs and an electronic database allowing for sophisticated searching and concordancing were developed at Brigham Young University in Provo, Utah. The Orion Center for the Study of Dead Sea Scrolls was founded at Hebrew University. A new journal, *Dead Sea Discoveries*, was launched by Brill Academic Publishers, complementing the longstanding *Revue de Qumran* (began 1955), and the International Organization of Qumran Studies was formed. Among the most important developments was the new cycle of public exhibitions of scrolls, begun by the Israel Antiquities Authority in 1993, continuing to the present, with more planned for the future.

Dating the Dead Sea Scrolls

As we have seen, there were disagreements about dating the scrolls from the moment they were discovered. The first scholars to see them did not recognize their antiquity

precisely because it is not an easy matter to date ancient documents, especially documents more than 2000 years old.

Since their discovery the scrolls have been dated by two methods. The first is called paleography, or the study of old writing. The changing styles of writing letters in the ancient world can be dated from documents whose age is known by other means, and a system of classifying the evolution of handwriting has been developed which allows scholars to date documents with some degree of accuracy to within about 25-50 years of their composition. Professors Albright and Cross were among the first to develop the system for ancient biblical manuscripts. Based on this typology of writing styles most of the scrolls from the Judean Desert fall within the range of 250 BC-135 CE, with those at Qumran ending about 50 CE.

The other method is radiocarbon dating. Arising out of atomic research at the University of Chicago during World War II, this dating method was applied to the linen coverings of the first scrolls almost immediately after their discovery. Found in all living organisms, carbon-14 is a radioactive isotope of carbon discovered in 1940. When an organism dies, its constituent carbon isotopes begin to decay. Half of the original isotope will decay into nitrogen-14 over a period of 5,730 years. By measuring the extent of such decay in the remains of ancient cloth or parchment or papyrus, it is possible to date, within a relatively small margin of error, the death of the plants and animals from which they were made.

At first, radiocarbon dating required burning (carbonizing) sizeable amounts of the material being tested. For this reason the cloth coverings associated with some of the scrolls from Qumran Cave 1 were used for dating, rather than the scrolls themselves.

During November 1950, three of the St. Mark's Scrolls (Isaiah, Habakkuk Commentary and Rule of the Community) were displayed at the University of Chicago together with some of their linen coverings. While these scrolls and wrappings were in Chicago, Prof. Carl Kraeling, associated with the Oriental Institute of the University of Chicago and the American Schools of Oriental Research, arranged for Prof. Willard Libby, also at the university, to perform a radiocarbon dating test. Libby's tests dated the flax used to produce the linen wrappings of the scrolls to about 33 CE, plus or minus 200 years, precisely during the Second Temple period and the lifetime of Jesus.

By the 1980s newer radiocarbon dating tests were developed. These tests required the destruction of much less material, so it became feasible to test the scrolls themselves. Such tests have been performed on a variety of scrolls over the past fifteen years. These tests have validated the earlier dates made on the basis of paleography, confirming conclusively the great antiquity of the Dead Sea Scrolls.

The Survival of the Dead Seas Scrolls, Past and Future

The survival of the Dead Sea Scrolls can be attributed to several factors. The use of parchment (dried animal skins) and leather (tanned animal skins), writing materials more durable than papyrus, was a crucial factor. Equally important was the climate of the region. The Judean Desert, and in particular, the area along the shores of the Dead Sea, is extremely dry. Furthermore, the caves proved to be the ideal place to store them for preservation. The caves not only protected the scrolls from the occasional winter rains, but were dark and isolated as well. The caves also moderated the outside temperature. They were cooler in the summer and warmer in the winter. Scrolls stored in jars fared the best. Those not in jars suffered more disintegration, but even these survived beyond anything conceivable or predictable until the first discoveries were made.

The first decades of scroll research were largely consumed with putting the pieces back together, categorizing, transcribing and deciphering. Little, however, was accomplished in the area of long-term conservation. The Israel Antiquities Authority set up a conservation laboratory during the early 1990s specifically to restore and, inasmuch as possible, preserve the scrolls for future generations. After more than a decade of work, it is estimated that it will take another twenty years or more to complete the process.

Archaeology and Qumran

The connection between the ruins of Khirbet Qumran and the scrolls suggested itself immediately. Half the scrolls caves were within just a few meters of the site, and the other scrolls caves in the area were within easy walking distance. The excavations of the site proved, at least to those who excavated, that those who preserved, copied, and to some extent, composed the scrolls were residents of Qumran.

Over the decades since de Vaux finished his investigations other archaeologists have put forward additional theories, among them that Qumran was simply a military fort, or that it, together with Ain Feshka, was an agricultural establishment, or that it was a factory of some sort, perhaps for pottery.

The majority of scholars, however, still connect Qumran with the scrolls. Excavations on the plateau near the ruins continue.

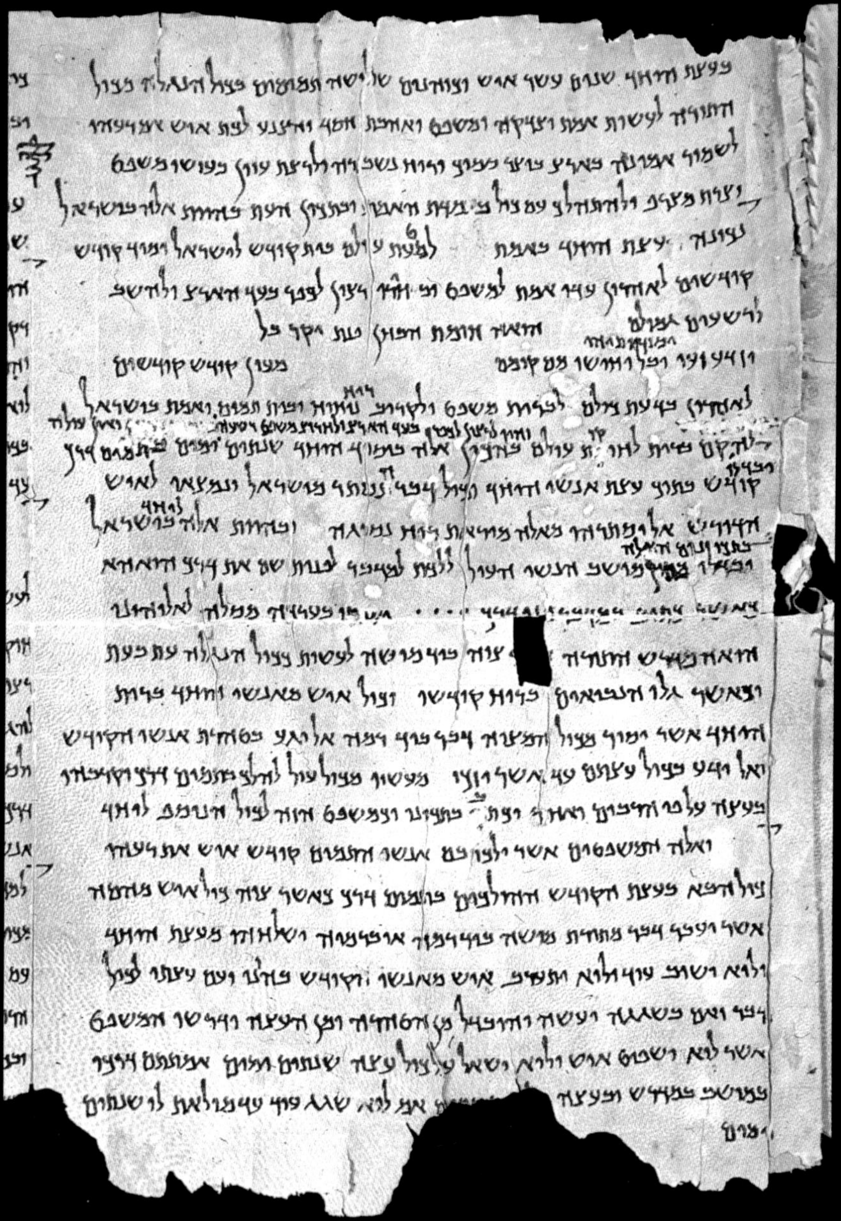

Manual of Discipline (1QS), Column 8, lines 1-4

1 In the Community council (there shall be) twelve men and three priests, perfect in everything that has been revealed from all

2 the law to implement truth, justice, judgment, compassionate love and unassuming behavior
of one to another,

3 to preserve faithfulness in the land with firm purpose and repentant spirit in order to atone
for sin by doing justice

4 and undergoing trials, and to walk with everyone in the measure of the truth and the regulation of the time.

(*The Dead Sea Scrolls Study Edition*, Vol. 1, ed.
and transl. by F. García Martínez and E.J.C.
Tigchelaar [Leiden: Brill, 1997])

View of Qumran from a cave high in the cliffs above, showing the escarpment of Cave 4. Richard T. Nowitz/Corbis

Chapter 3

THE DEAD SEA SCROLLS
AND THE BIBLE

The Great Isaiah Scroll (1Q-Isaiahᵃ), column 28, containing Isaiah 34:1-36:2. © John C. Trever/Corbis

When scholars found biblical texts among the more than 2000-year-old Dead Sea Scrolls the implications for the history of the Bible were immediately clear. Until this discovery there had been a gap of approximately 1200 years between the writing of the last book of the Hebrew Bible and the oldest surviving Hebrew manuscript of any part of it. Older translations in other languages had survived, but nothing in Hebrew itself. The scrolls narrowed that gap to about 200 years or less.

The books of the Hebrew Bible were transmitted from generation to generation over thousands of years by scribes who painstakingly copied everything by hand. Over the centuries textual variants, or differences between manuscripts in wording or spelling, naturally occurred. Undoubtedly there were intentional changes along the way as well. All this resulted in different streams of textual tradition, but the differences were relatively minor.

These different streams of textual traditions are represented in the scrolls found side by side at Qumran and elsewhere in the Judean Desert. In some cases the scrolls have even helped recover parts of the text previously lost. But taken as a whole, the scrolls show that the Bible used in the time of the Second Temple, during the lifetime of Jesus, was basically the same one passed down through the ages until today. The differences are neither theologically nor historically important. In general the scrolls testify to the amazing accuracy and great care with which ancient scribes passed along the biblical text.

But what is the Bible, how did it come to be gathered together, and how did it come into our hands today? The Jewish Scriptures are also known as the Hebrew Bible, or the Old Testament. For Christians Scripture is a combination of the Old Testament and the New Testament. The various books of the Hebrew Bible were written over a period of years by various authors. Many Jews and Christians believe that God himself inspired the writers of the Bible, in some presently inscrutable way controlling their compositions while at the same time not effacing their individual styles.

How particular compositions or books came to be considered inspired or worthy to be part of a growing collection of holy books is shrouded in mystery. In many cases even the authorship of a book is difficult to trace after so many centuries, for very often a biblical book does not itself indicate who wrote it. But some books came to be generally accepted as more special or valuable than others, and eventually, Jewish communities came to accept these as inspired, to be distinguished from other books which were useful, but somehow did not have the same divine imprint upon them.

The fluidity of the collection can be illustrated by imagining a storage room in the Jerusalem Temple where official copies of various Jewish scrolls were kept. On one side of the room were shelves with the holy books.

On the other side of the room were shelves for other, less holy books. In those days there were only individual scrolls for books, (such as the book of Genesis) or scrolls combining a few books (such as the Torah or books of Moses). The "codex" form, a series of pages bound together to make what we think of today as a "book," was a later invention.

In this situation, with individual scrolls, it would have been simple to transfer a particular scroll from one side of the room to the other, if a consensus of authorities allowed it. Thus, in the days of scrolls instead of bound codices, it was easy for the collection of holy books to shrink or expand. It should be noted that we do not know for certain that there was such a room. But we do know for sure that the "Bible" at that time would have been *a collection of different scrolls*. More than this, the Dead Sea Scrolls seem to indicate that the collection now known as the Hebrew Bible was not yet completely closed during the Second Temple period, when Christianity began and the Qumran Community was at its height.

Among the Dead Sea Scrolls we find multiple copies of certain books. The biblical books of Psalms, Isaiah and Deuteronomy appear most frequently from among the books that came to comprise the Hebrew Bible. These three books are also the most quoted books in the New Testament. But we also find among the Dead Sea Scrolls multiple copies of other books that did not find their way into the collection eventually known as the Bible.

It is uncertain exactly what can be

deduced from the phenomenon of multiple copies. It might be logical to assume that books copied five times or ten or twenty times had a special significance to the community at Qumran or the larger Jewish community, but that is not the only possible conclusion. Any book could be copied more than once for a variety of reasons, some of which we might not even know or be able to imagine. And survival of multiple copies for a particular book might have been random or accidental. Nevertheless, it is generally believed today that the more copies of a book found in the Qumran caves, the more likely people there considered them holy or canonical (measuring up to a particular standard and thus worthy of inclusion in the Bible), although the whole idea of a fixed list of accepted books was actually a later development in both Judaism and Christianity.

Sometime during the first two centuries CE there was a standardization of the biblical Hebrew text, or a least the choice of a particular textual stream as preferable. Some scholars trace this to the Council of Jamnia in 90. Other scholars question whether the decision was made there, or even whether there was ever a single decision at all. As we have said, slightly different versions of the Hebrew books had been used by Jewish communities everywhere for centuries, and the people at Qumran were no different. But little by little there came to be a preferred text, and today this is known as the Masoretic or traditional text of the Hebrew Bible, a prominent text type in the Dead Sea Scrolls as well.

Nevertheless, various stages and several streams of the transmission of the biblical text are represented among the scrolls. For this reason the scrolls can occasionally clarify difficulties or ambiguities, and sometimes even have enabled the restoration of parts of the Hebrew text which had been lost over the centuries. Just one example will demonstrate the value of the scrolls in this respect.

Among the 150 psalms or songs gathered together in the Bible there is a particular type, known as "acrostics." An acrostic psalm is so named because each succeeding verse begins with the next letter of the alphabet. In English terms, this would mean that the first verse begins with "a," the second with "b," the third with "c," and so on. Psalm 145 is such an acrostic. Verse by verse it follows the alphabet until verse 14, which should have started with the Hebrew letter equivalent to "n." But the first part of the verse is missing, and in Hebrew verse 14 starts with the next letter of the alphabet, equivalent to English "s." The missing verse had survived in the Septuagint, the Greek translation of the Hebrew Bible (Old Testament), produced for the Jewish community in Alexandria, Egypt about 250 BC. This translation was popular in the time of Jesus and was adopted by many early Christians as their "Old Testament."

Thus, it had been known for centuries that something was missing and the Greek translation filled it in. But what was not clear was how the Greek translators had come up with the missing first part of the verse. Had they simply made up something appropriate to complete the acrostic, or were they translating from a Hebrew manuscript containing the complete verse? The Dead Sea Scrolls solved the mystery. In one of the copies of Psalms from Qumran the complete verse appears, proving that it was originally known in Hebrew and that the Greek translators worked from a manuscript containing it. The verse has now been included in many modern translations, including, for example, the *New International Version*: "The LORD is faithful in all his promises and loving toward all he has made."

Phylacteries

Among the many criticisms Jesus made of the Pharisees in Matthew 23 is a reference to phylacteries in verse 5: "Everything they do is done for men to see: They make their phylacteries wide and the tassels on their garments long." A phylactery was a capsule containing small strips of parchment on which were written passages from Deuteronomy and Exodus. A capsule affixed to a doorpost is a *mezuza* and those attached to the forehead or left arm during prayer are *tefillin*. A number of these small parchments for such capsules were found at Qumran in Caves 4 and 8, some of them containing more extended passages of Scripture than are ordinarily used by Jews today.

The Non-biblical Dead Sea Scrolls

About two-thirds of the Dead Sea Scrolls consist of non-biblical Jewish literature, illuminating both Jewish life in Second Temple times and many aspects of Christianity and the New Testament. Among the works surviving in the scrolls one finds a variety of types of literature.

Two of the books of the Apocrypha, or Deutero-canonical (second canon) books, are found among the scrolls: Sirach (Ecclesiasticus) and Tobit. Probably known at Qumran because they were older than the other books of the "Old Testament Apocrypha," these books have been accepted as Scripture by various Jewish and Christian groups through the ages, and are found today in the Christian Catholic Bible, but not the Protestant.

There are also pseudepigraphical books purportedly written by famous historical figures who did not actually write them. Such names as Enoch, Noah, Abraham, Moses, Job, Joshua, David, Solomon, Daniel, and Ezra were associated with works as a literary stamp of approval. Two such books were favorites at Qumran, Jubilees, and Enoch. Jubilees deals mainly with the true calendar, a matter of considerable importance to the Qumran community who adhered to the older 364-day solar calendar. Written in Aramaic, the book of Enoch is a collection of apocalypses dealing with a variety of subjects such as angels and the calendar.

Other scrolls were preserved, but not necessarily originally composed, by the sect at Qumran. An example is the Temple Scroll, apparently meant to be an addition to the Torah. It presents an updated version of the law in Deuteronomy as well as a blueprint for the Temple in Jerusalem. Two copies were found in Cave 11, one fairly well preserved, which is the longest of the Dead Sea Scrolls, and an older one, much less well preserved.

Originally called the book of Lamech, the Aramaic Genesis Apocyphron resembles to an extent some of today's expanded Bible storybooks. It embellishes the patriarchal narratives of Genesis and makes use of the book of Jubilees mentioned above.

Another work of particular importance to the community at Qumran is known today as the "Songs of the Sabbath Sacrifice." It describes the classes of angels responsible for the heavenly worship service on thirteen consecutive Sabbaths, one quarter of the year. This book is notable because it was discovered not only in Qumran Caves 4 and 11, but also at Masada.

And there are biblical commentaries of various types, the most prominent of which are the *pesherim*, commentaries on Scripture often but not always consisting of interpretations with references to events in the writer's own time, the recent past, or the near future. Commentaries were found at Qumran on Isaiah, Micah, Zephaniah, Psalms, Hosea, Nahum, and Habakkuk.

Several copies of a scroll known as the War Rule also survived at Qumran. This work describes a future decisive battle between the forces of the "sons of light and the sons of darkness," good and evil. The terminology is notable since it also appears in the New Testament.

One of the most important types of literature deals specially with the Qumranites themselves and their own rules for conduct. Various forms of these prescriptions are known as the *Rule of the Community* (1QS, first part), the *Manual of Discipline* (1QS, second part), the Rule of the Congregation (1QS^a) and the Rule of Blessings (1QS^b).

The *Damascus Document* or New Covenant in the land of Damascus was first known from the Cairo Genizah, discovered at the end of the nineteenth century in the Karaite synagogue. It is an extensive document detailing legal regulations and a revised version of the *Manual of Discipline*. Some have even called it an early form of the Mishnah.

If one goes beyond the Qumran collection to include all the scrolls of the Judean Desert, many of the kinds of documents one would expect from everyday life have survived: marriage and divorce contracts, commercial and military documents, and personal letters.

Testimonia (4Q175), lines 1-8

1 And **** spoke to Moses saying: Deut 5:28-29 "You have heard the sound of the words of

2 this people, what they said to you: all they have said is right.

3 If (only) it were given (that) they had /this/ heart to fear me and keep all

4 my precepts all the days, so that it might go well with them and their sons forever!"

5 Deut 18:18-19 "I would raise up for them a prophet from among their brothers, like you, and place my words

6 in his mouth, and he would tell them all that I command him. And it will happen that /the/ man

7 who does not listen to my words which the prophet will speak in my name, I

8 shall require a reckoning from him." *Blank*

(*The Dead Sea Scrolls Study Edition*, Vol. 1, ed. and transl. by F. García Martínez and E.J.C. Tigchelaar [Leiden: Brill, 1997])

Tower among the excavated ruins at Qumran predating the settlement in the second century BCE.

Chapter 4

THE DEAD SEA SCROLLS,
JUDAISM, AND CHRISTIANITY

Selection from the Habakkuk Commentary (Pesher Habakkuk, 1QpeshHab), Column 8. © John C. Trever

Because the scrolls are Jewish, were written in the land of the Bible, and many date to the same general era when Jesus lived and taught, it is not surprising that soon after their discovery scholars began to make comparisons and connections between the scrolls, Judaism and Christianity.

These relationships have often been explored separately: "the scrolls and Judaism" or "the scrolls and Christianity." But a good case can be made for considering them all together. Jesus was a Jewish rabbi or teacher (John 3:2) and all Christians until the Jerusalem Council in 45 CE were Jewish (Acts 15:1-33). Jesus' Jewish disciples believed he was the Messiah. The early Christians saw no contradiction between their Jewishness and their belief in Jesus' death as an atoning sacrifice for their sins, nor their belief in his resurrection as a guarantee and precursor of their own everlasting life.

Put differently, early Christianity was a Jewish sect—one of several in that time and place. The New Testament was written largely by Jews for Jews, and the Gospels, especially, are best understood even today when viewed through a Jewish lens. Early Christians struggled with the question of accepting Gentiles, and only as Christianity grew and spread did it become a faith for all, Jewish and Gentile alike: "to the Jews first, and also to the Greek" (Romans 1:16). With this shared background then, it is only to be expected that the Dead Sea

Scrolls have illuminated both Judaism before destruction of the Second Temple (70 CE) and Christianity and the New Testament.

First, the scrolls have given us detailed information about a Jewish sect calling itself the *Yahad*, the "group." Many scholars have identified this group with a sect already known from antiquity, the Essenes. Whatever its name or affiliation, the picture we get of this Jewish group from the scrolls is fairly clear. It was a group that had separated itself from the dominant leadership in Jerusalem. It was meticulous in its observance of the law and even added its own regulations for daily life in its community. The group emphasized the study of Scripture and produced commentaries that interpreted the Hebrew Bible in terms of prophecies fulfilled in its own day. The sect was expecting a Messiah, or possibly two, and a future decisive battle between the forces of good and evil. It was fascinated with apocalyptic books such as Enoch, but its most copied books were Deuteronomy, Isaiah, and the Psalms. The group adhered to an older calendar, putting it at odds with Jerusalem over the timing of all the major celebrations and holidays. The community shared its goods, required a period of probation for membership, and maintained its worship without recourse to the Temple in Jerusalem. Still, it was thoroughly Jewish. No one would have doubted that.

But what about John the Baptist, Jesus, his disciples, and the New Testament? They were also thoroughly Jewish and yet separate, eventually, from the dominant forms of Judaism represented by the leaders in Jerusalem. Was there any connection at all between the group at Qumran whom we know from the Dead Sea Scrolls and pre-Christian and Christian leaders and their writings? Far from being feared, such connections, could they be established, would be welcomed by many Christians because they could be so instructive. But are they really there?

One may approach this question from several directions. First, one may consider *chronology* and *geography*. From the standpoint of time and place, there is the possibility that John the Baptist, Jesus, the first disciples, and other early Christians at least *knew* about the group at Qumran. John baptized Jesus in the Jordan river, not far from Qumran. Jesus taught in Jericho. It is almost certain that both also would have known about the larger community of Essenes in Jerusalem and elsewhere, as described by Josephus and others, whether the group at Qumran is identified with the Essenes or not. Knowledge of a group, even physical contact, however, does not necessarily imply influence. Likewise, lack of knowledge does not guarantee lack of influence. We may trace apparent similarities between groups much more easily than we can discover how these similarities came to be. It is perhaps most important to look not so much at influence as at similarities, and to try to understand what such similarities mean.

An important factor for trying to understand the possible relationship between the New Testament, Christianity, Second Temple Judaism, and the Dead Sea Scrolls is shared religious *terminology*. For someone familiar with the New Testament certain terms almost jump off the pages of the scrolls. The special meanings given to words and phrases like "mystery," "flesh," "spirit," "power," "truth," "sons of light and sons of darkness," "Belial," "everlasting fire," "spirit of holiness," "light of life," "prince of lights," "angel of darkness," "crown of glory," "abyss of darkness," "judgment," "Most High," "sons of heaven," "the many" (= "group" or "congregation"), "works of the law", "a voice crying in the wilderness," and others, immediately suggest connections. Some of this one would expect. After all, everyone in question was Jewish, the Hebrew Bible was the literary basis of their life and faith, and they lived more or less in the same time and place. Still, the similarities of terminology and outlook are striking. Whatever else all this means, at least it shows that the Gospels especially, but also the entire New Testament, are authentic representations of the Jewish literary, cultural, religious, and linguistic environment in the Land in the first century.

Another factor is shared *practice.* There were many differences of social behavior and religious practice between the various sects of Judaism in that day, just as there are now. However, there is one arresting similarity between the early Christians in Jerusalem and the group at Qumran: the sharing of property or "community of goods." It is well known from the New Testament book of Acts that at least in Jerusalem Christians shared their goods. To what extent this was localized

and temporary is difficult to conclude, and the practice, only partly successful, faded out rather quickly as Christianity spread. Nevertheless, that it appeared at all at the very time and so close to the place the same sort of thing was practiced in Qumran seizes one's attention. When a new member passed his two year probation period at Qumran and was accepted into the community, he was required to hand over all his possessions to be shared among all the members, much as one might expect today in a monastery.

On the other hand, "community of goods" and even the disdain for "riches" among both was more a social than a religious convention, and it is perhaps most important to draw the same conclusion again: this similarity between the group at Qumran and early Christians in Jerusalem shows that the New Testament reflects the time and place it claims to; the similarity does not necessarily prove any direct influence or connection. In both cases, in fact, it may simply be a reflection of economic necessity: if they were to survive, both early Christians and the group at Qumran had to share their worldly goods.

Another similarity between early Christianity and the group of the Dead Sea Scrolls is a shared outlook about God's sovereignty, or God's control over the course of events in the universe. The degree to which the New Testament teaches predestination or foreordination is still an inner-Christian argument. But it is patently clear that the Dead Sea Scrolls mean to teach predestination. Such expressions as "God's Plan" and the "Eternal Plan" are used in a way that leads inevitably to the conclusion that the sect at Qumran believed that God had planned their lives down to the smallest details. This is the reason that they could decide everything by lot—including who would be allowed into the group. They had confidence that God determined the outcome when they threw the dice. Nevertheless, just as in the New Testament, individuals were held responsible for their choices, the overarching plan of a sovereign God notwithstanding.

A point of both similarity and dissimilarity between the people of the scrolls and Christians was the matter of repentance and conversion. Both groups strongly believed in the necessity of conversion, but the nature of the conversion was vastly different. At Qumran the conversion consisted of a commitment to keep the law, and more particularly, the rules of the community. After a period of two years during which the actions of the candidate were watched, he would be baptized, allowed into the community, and given certain preliminary privileges. By way of contrast, Christian conversion, while also signified by baptism, was instantaneous, and carried with it an emphasis on the *spirit* of the law, a deep and profound inner "circumcision of the heart."

The groups also had an entirely different sort of origin. Christianity emerged around a person with a name, with known parents, a known birthplace, disciples with names who came from and lived in known places. Its manner and time of origin are known. By contrast, we know nothing precisely of the original leader of the Dead Sea Scrolls Sect, when the break from Jerusalem was made,

or when the community at Qumran was begun. It is true that all this was undoubtedly known by the Qumranites, and had more of their literature survived we might be able to fill in some of those blanks. But the lack of personal details at Qumran is as notable as it is mysterious.

An even more prominent difference is the matter of resurrection. Not only does Christianity claim that its founder, Jesus, died and was resurrected, it also looks forward to a resurrection from the dead for all believers. The latter was certainly a tenet of several Jewish groups in Jesus' day, but there is nothing at Qumran comparable to Jesus' death and resurrection.

There are other differences too. Jesus used parables extensively in his teaching, something that we do not find at Qumran. Jesus claimed to be the Messiah (Greek = "Christ," "anointed") and Son of God. Jesus was an itinerant rabbi, while the leader at Qumran was probably a priest and seems to have been more sedentary. Jesus reached out to anyone who would listen, while the group at Qumran seems to have been largely concerned with itself. The New Testament claims Jesus performed supernatural miracles, but there is no record of such at Qumran. Jesus promised to return again after he ascended into heaven, but there is neither an ascension nor an eschatological return posited for any leaders of the Dead Sea Sect. In Christianity there was no original hierarchical or social distinction between pastors and lay people, but at Qumran there seems to have been a fairly rigid social and organizational hierarchy.

Jesus and his disciples deliberately broke small technicalities of the Sabbath to make a point ("the Sabbath was made for man, not man for the Sabbath"), but Sabbath practice at Qumran was considerably more restrictive than even the biblical law prescribed. Jesus participated in festivals and ceremonies in the Jerusalem Temple, as did early Christians, but the people at Qumran maintained little or no connection with the Temple at all.

This rather random sampling of the differences and similarities between these two Jewish groups, the sect of the Dead Sea Scrolls and early Christianity, shows that while they shared a common background and while the scrolls can indeed enable us to understand many things about Christianity and the New Testament, it is highly unlikely there was any organic connection or direct influence between or among them.

©Bruce Zuckerman/Corbis

Rule of the Congregation (1QS^a), Column 1, lines 1-5

1 And this is the rule of all the congregation of Israel in the final days, when they gather [in community to wa]lk

2 in accordance with the regulation of the sons of Zadok, the priests, and the men of their covenant who have turn[ed away from the] path

3 of the nation. These are the men of his counsel who have kept his covenant in the midst of wickedness to ato[ne for the ear]th.

4 When they come, they shall assemble all those who come, including children and women, and they shall read into [their] ea[rs]

5 [a]ll the precepts of the covenant, and shall instruct them in all their regulations, so that they do not stray in [the]ir e[rrors.]

(*The Dead Sea Scrolls Study Edition*, Vol. 1, ed. and transl. by F. García Martínez and E.J.C. Tigchelaar [Leiden: Brill, 1997])

The escarpment containing Cave 4 at Qumran with Wadi Qumran to the left.

Chapter 5

QUMRAN AND THE ESSENES

The Jewish sect at Qumran was connected to the Essenes soon after the discovery of the scrolls, first by Sowmy, his brother, and Mar Samuel; then by Sukenik; later by Trever, Brownlee, Burrows; and finally by most other scholars since. It is a hypothesis that continues to be vigorously defended, although there are several competing identifications.

Information about the Essenes comes from a few ancient sources, the most prolific of which was Josephus,

Just behind Cave 4 at Qumran. Photo from the plateau next to the main settlement, showing the close proximity to the two. Oleg Kantor/Shutterstock

the famous Jewish general and historian (37-101 CE) who wrote his history of the Jewish Wars and Jewish People under the patronage of the Romans some years after their destruc-

tion of the Temple in 70 CE and Masada in 73 CE. As a young man Josephus briefly trained to be an Essene, living in the wilderness with Bannus (an Essene?) for three years. He also studied as a Sadducee, but ended up attached to the Pharisees, perhaps more as a matter of political and social expediency than religious belief. The sect is not mentioned in the New Testament.

Over the years since the discovery of the Dead Sea Scrolls descriptions of Essene life from Josephus have come to be mixed with descriptions of the life of the *Yahad* at Qumran to such an extent that many people today are no longer able to distinguish between the various sources. This mixture and confusion are understandable. If one accepted the conclusion that the Qumranites were Essenes, why not use Josephus' more complete descriptions of the sect to fill out the picture? This has resulted in a composite view of life at Qumran which might be more or less correct, but should still be recognized as composite, because there are also striking differences between the Essenes described by Josephus (as well as Pliny the Elder and Philo of Alexandria) and the people at Qumran.

I have thought it would be helpful to present a brief summary of the sources themselves. This summary shows that if the Qumranites were a branch of the Essenes, they were apparently somewhat different from the branch described by Josephus and others. It is true that one must always allow for differences between rules and practices. What was prescribed in Qumran literature might not have been precisely practiced. Furthermore, even within a single religious group practices change from time to time and place to place. Yet it is only fair to present both similarities and differences in the ongoing effort to construct a description of the people at Qumran.

The Essenes as Described by Josephus in his Jewish Wars

Most of what Josephus has to say about the Essenes comes from his *Jewish Wars*. Again, the following summary of Josephus' description may have been characteristic of the group at Qumran, but only if one assumes that they were Essenes of some sort.

Josephus speaks of a man named "Judas the Essene," a teacher "who never made a prophecy which did not come true." He says the Essenes had disciples, cultivated personal piety and were strongly attached to each other. The Essenes shunned pleasures and regarded temperance and self-control as special virtues. He reports that some married and some didn't. Those who did gave their wives a three-month probation period (engagement) during which they had to show the possibility of fertility by having three menstrual periods. There was no sex before marriage or during pregnancy. The Essenes adopted other men's children while young and pliable in order to teach their own principles. The ones who did not marry did not condemn wedlock, but wished to "protect themselves from women's wantonness, being convinced that no woman keeps her promise to one man."

New members, Josephus reports, donated all their possessions to the community upon admission. There was neither poverty nor inordinate wealth in their communities. They considered oil defiling and therefore were known for their dry skin. They always dressed in white. They elected their leaders and the assembly of the sect determined its leaders' duties.

They did not occupy one particular town, for there were "large numbers in every town." Any Essene traveling from city to city had all the resources of the group at his disposal wherever he went, so they took nothing for a journey except arms. In every city one of the order was expressly appointed to attend to strangers, providing them with all necessities, even clothes. They dressed and acted "like children under rigorous discipline." They did not change their garments or shoes until they were torn to shreds or worn threadbare with age. There was no buying or selling among themselves: they exchanged goods only, but they were also permitted to take anything from any of their brothers without compensation in return.

Before the sun was up they uttered no word on mundane matters, but offered prayers inherited from their forefathers as though entreating the sun to rise. After prayers, their superiors assigned them to various crafts in which they were proficient, and they worked strenuously until the "fifth hour" (11:00 a.m.?). At the fifth hour they gathered together, tied linen cloths around their waists, and bathed their bodies in cold water. After this they assembled in a private room, where none of the uninitiated could enter. Then they went to the dining hall and the baker served bread to each one on a plate. Before eating the priest said grace and no one ate before the prayer. After breakfast he offered another prayer.

After changing clothes they went back to work until evening. For the evening meal they ate in a similar manner, as did guests, presumably other initiated Essenes. No clamor or disturbance ever polluted their dwellings. They spoke in turn, none interrupting his neighbor. To outsiders their silence appeared like some awful mystery, but it was due to their invariable sobriety and the limitation of their allotted portions of food and drink to what they needed only.

In all other matters they did nothing without orders from their superiors. Only two things were left to individual discretion: rendering of assistance and compassion. Presents to relatives were forbidden, unless allowed by the leaders. They were masters of their tempers, champions of fidelity, ambassadors of peace. Any promise of theirs had more force than an oath—swearing they avoided because one who cannot be believed without an appeal to God stands condemned already.

They displayed an extraordinary interest in the writings of the ancients. They were partcularly interested in writings which spoke to the welfare of both the soul and the body and thus made investigations into medicinal roots and the properties of minerals.

Admission to the sect was not immediate: there was a three year probation period. They made a long list of promises upon entering the sect. Anyone convicted of a serious infraction was expelled, but often restored. They were a secret order and their secrets were passed along orally from member to member. They promised to transmit the rules exactly as they had received them.

They never passed a sentence in a court of less than a hundred members. After God they revered Moses the most, and anyone who criticized Moses could be punished by death. They obeyed their elders and majority decisions of the members.

They did not spit in company or to the right (see also the Jerusalem Talmud). They were the strictest ·sabbatarians. They did not defecate on the Sabbath, nor even take the dishes from the table. They dug holes a foot deep to defecate on other days, and immediately buried it and afterwards washed their hands.

They were divided into four grades. The senior members were so far superior to the junior members that if touched by a junior the senior would take a bath, just as after contact with a stranger.

Most Essenes lived to be at least 100 from the simplicity and regularity of their lives. They made light of danger and triumphed over pain by their resolute will. Some of their number professed to tell the future, and they were seldom wrong.

The Essenes as Described by Josephus in his Jewish Antiquities

In his *Jewish Antiquities* Josephus adds a few more details:

The Essenes believed that Fate is the mistress of all things, and that nothing befalls men unless it be in accordance with her decree. They followed the teachings of Pythagoras, and were specially honored by Herod the Great, because one of them named Menachem (Greek: Manaemus) prophesied that Herod would be king while he was still a child.

Josephus repeats that the Essenes were known as prophets (Simon the Essene). The Essenes sent votive offerings to the temple, but performed their own sacrifices employing a different ritual of purification. They were therefore barred from the temple precincts, performing the rites themselves.

The Essenes taught that one should rely on God in all things, that the soul was immortal and that it was necessary to struggle to obtain the reward of righteousness.

They devoted themselves solely to agricultural labor and were more virtuous in Josephus' eyes than any other group. There were more than 4000 altogether in the country. They did not bring wives to the community, nor did they own slaves. Instead, they performed menial tasks for each other. They elected their leaders by a show of hands.

The Essenes as Described by Philo of Alexandria, "That Every Good Man is Free"

Philo Judaeus of Alexandria (about 30 BC-40 CE) adds more details about the Essenes. According to him they were utterly dedicated to the service of God, but they did not offer animal sacrifice, judging it more important to render their minds holy. They avoided large cities because of the ungodliness customary there. They were both farmers and craftsmen. They did not hoard money, were not large landowners, and lived "without goods and property," because they considered frugality and contentment to be most important. They did not produce arms or even peaceful objects that could be used for violence. They did not engage in business. No slaves were used by the Essenes because they considered all men equal.

The Essenes did not spend time on philosophy, but emphasized ethics and their ancestral laws. They studied Scripture every day, but especially on the Sabbath. They sat in the synagogues according to their age, the young men below the old. In their synagogues one would read the text and another would explain it, giving instruction by means of symbols. They emphasized piety, holiness, justice, and correct behavior. They rejected oaths, falsehood, and emphasized virtues. They had a communal life in which there was no private ownership. They welcomed Essene guests freely. They took good care of their sick and respected the aged. Philo calls them "athletes of virtue." No ruler was ever able to lay a charge against them.

The Essenes as Described by Philo of Alexandria, "In Defense of the Jews"

The Essenes lived in "a number of towns in Judaea," but also in many villages and large groups. People enlisted in the sect out of a zeal for virtue, so there were no young children, adolescents or young men. Rather, the group consisted of older men who were more stable, past being carried away by passions. Their lifestyle was completely communal in every way. They worked hard no matter what the weather, beginning before sunrise and ending after sunset. They considered hard work useful for both the body and soul. Among them were farmers, shepherds, and beekeepers as well as tradesmen. Any wages or salary earned was turned over to a steward who bought necessities for the group. They had both a common table and common clothes—heavy coats for winter and thin tunics for summer. Any illness was treated at the expense of the community. They banned marriage as well as sexual relations. Their lifestyle and character was so admirable that even great kings heaped "favors and honors" on them.

The Essenes as Described by Pliny the Elder in his **Natural History**

Pliny the Elder (Gaius Plinius Secundus, 23/24-79 CE) was a Roman gentleman from northern Italy. He compiled his work from over 100 authors and probably did not have a first-hand knowledge of either Judaea or the Essenes. The passage about the Essenes seems to have been composed after the destruction of the Second Temple of Jerusalem in 70 CE.

Still, we can glean a few details from him. The Essenes about which he writes lived to the west of the Dead Sea. They were unique and admired. They did not have women, but only palm trees for company. Large numbers of newcomers kept joining the sect, repenting of their past lives. "Below," (south) of the Essenes was En Gedi, at one time quite fertile and from there, continuing south was Masada.

Differences between Josephus and the Scrolls

Having taken under consideration Josephus' description of the Essenes, it must be pointed out, however, that there are some differences between his description and the picture that emerges from the Dead Sea Scrolls concerning the sect at Qumran.

The settlement at Qumran could not have accommodated more than a few hundred people at most, so Josephus' suggestion of 4000 altogether would have applied to the whole country, if, indeed the Qumranites were Essenes. We find nothing about working with crafts at Qumran, though the archaeological excavations might indicate that to some degree. The War Scroll does not sound very peaceful, but the eschatological situation they envisioned might have been viewed as a special circumstance. There is no mention at Qumran of white clothing specifically and exclusively. At least in one way of interpreting things, the people at Qumran made provision for wives and children. Some archaeologists connect what appear to be bones of women and children with the group at Qumran, but this is not certain. According to Josephus, admission to the group took three years, but in Qumran literature the probation period is two years. There is no mention in Qumran literature of daily bathing at Qumran, no prayers to the sun, and oaths do seem to have been used. There is no aversion to oil, for the "oil of anointing" is mentioned in the War Scroll. The seating arrangements at Qumran were by rank and not by age as in Philo's description, whereas at Qumran the seating arrangement was changed annually by examination. There is no evidence of "triple definitions" at Qumran, and a minimal use of symbols in their interpretations. There is no mention of a special interest in or knowledge of healing, roots or minerals

5-1 Looking north from the Qumran excavation toward the sites of Caves 1, 2, 3, and 11 in the cliffs. © John C. Trever

at Qumran. No expert prophets are named, nor is there any direct statement about veneration of Moses. Finally, there is no mention at Qumran of a council or court of 100 men. The number seems to have been 15.

Nevertheless, these seeming differences may be just that–seeming. Furthermore, evidence against an Essene identity based on the the lack of some provisions one might have expected to see in the literature of Qumran is not very strong, for there are several possible explanations for such missing material. Thus, while some of the differences are notable, for some even jarring, the scholarly consensus remains that the people of the Dead Sea Scrolls were Essenes of some sort.

11QPsalms, Column 21 lines 1–10
(Psalm 138:1-8, from the *Jerusalem Bible*)

1   138:1 Of David. I thank you,

2   Yahweh, with all my heart, In the presence of the angels I play for you, 138:2 and bow down

3   towards your holy Temple. I give thanks to your name for your love and faithfulness

4   your promise is even greater than your fame. 138:3 The day I called for help, your heard me

5   and you increased my strength. 138:4 Yahweh, all kings on earth give thanks to you, for they have heard your promises;

6   138:5 they celebrate Yahweh's actions, 'Great is the glory of Yahweh!'

7   138:6 From far above, Yahweh sees the humble, from far away he marks down the arrogant. 138:7 Though I live

8   surrounded by trouble, you keep me alive-to my enemies' fury! You stretch your hand out and save me,

9   138:8 your right hand will do everything for me. Yahweh, your love is everlasting,

10 do not abandon us whom you have made.

Courtesy of the Israel Antiquities Authority/Bruce Zuckerman

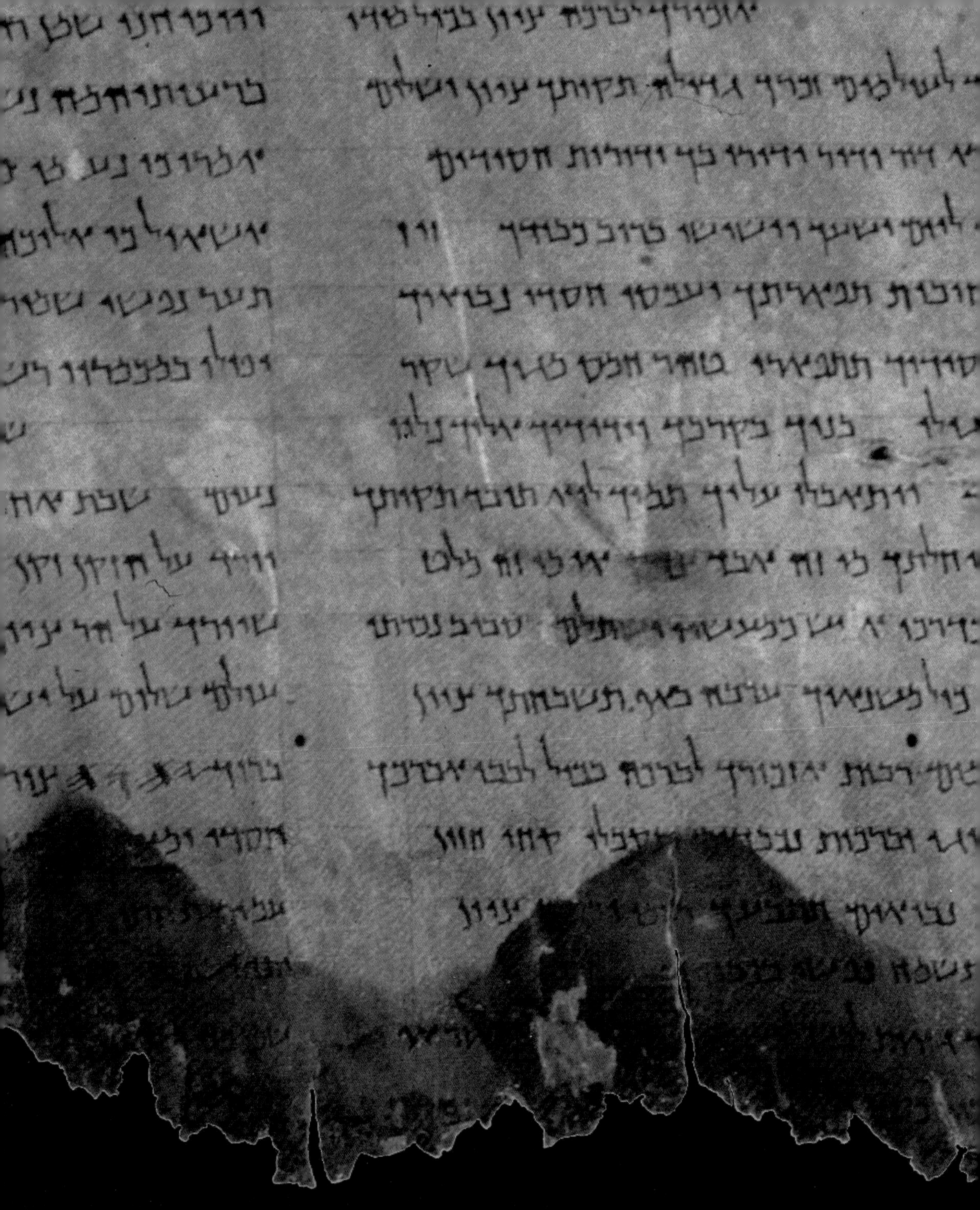

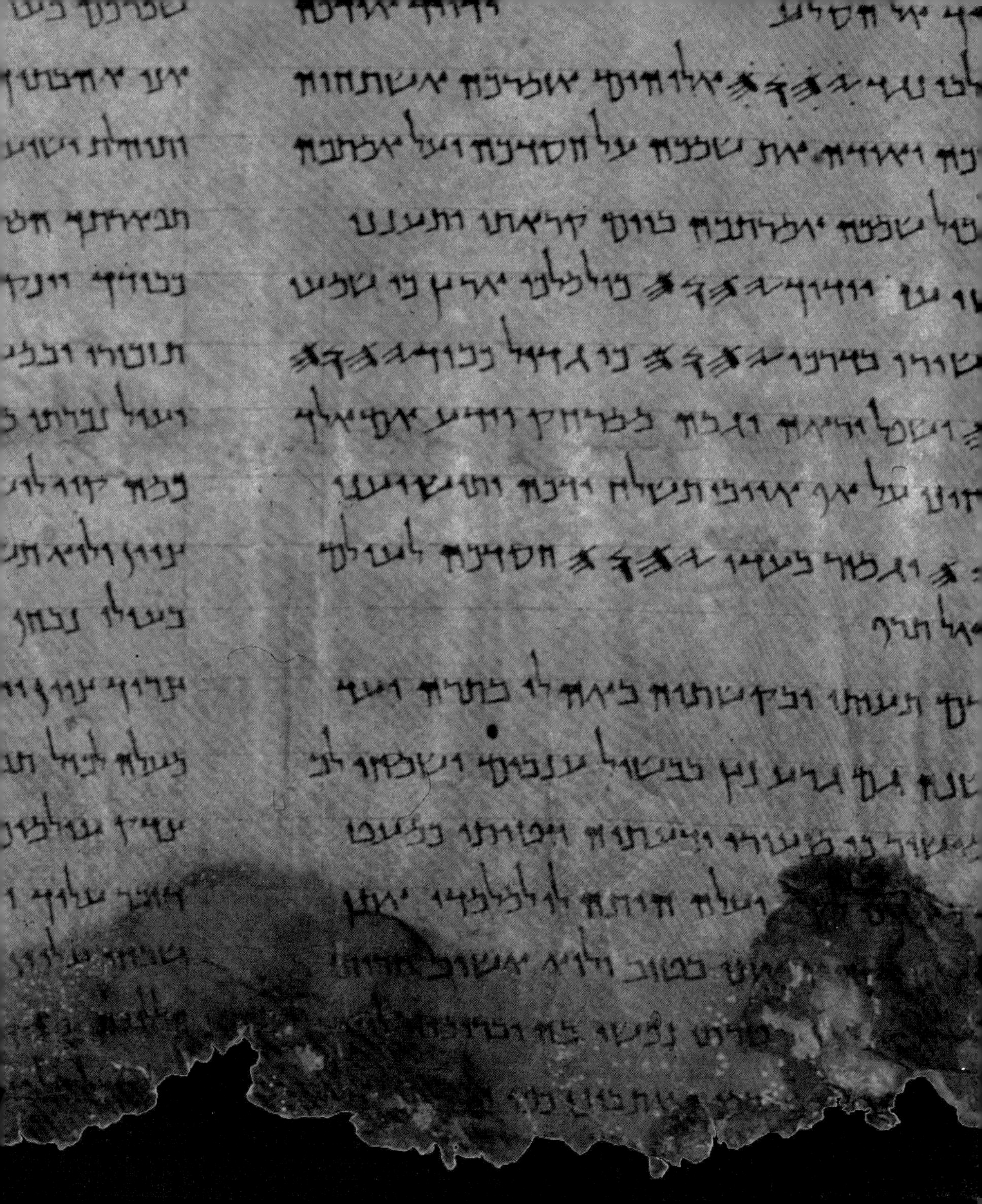

Aerial view of the excavation at Qumran, with Cave 4 in escarpment to the left. Richard T. Nowitz/Corbis

TIMELINE OF EVENTS
RELATED TO THE DEAD SEA SCROLLS

BCE (BC)

circa 250
• Oldest Dead Sea Scroll copied

circa 160/100
• Qumran Community founded.

circa 100
• The Great Isaiah Scroll (Isaiahᵃ) copied.

63
• The Roman General Pompeus occupies Palestine (Israel).

31
• Severe earthquake results in temporary abandonment of Qumran.

CE (AD)

30
• John the Baptist is teaching in the Jordan Valley near Qumran.

68
• Qumran is destroyed/abandoned.

70
• Jerusalem Temple is looted and destroyed by the Romans.

73
• Masada is captured by the Romans.

circa 217
• Scrolls are found in a jar in a cave near Jericho. The Church Father Origen uses one of these in his Hexapla, a six-column compilation of the Old Testament in parallel columns, five in Greek and one in Hebrew.

circa 800

- Timotheus, Patriarch of Seleucia in Isauria (present south central Turkey), mentions manuscripts found in a cave near Jericho. Several medieval authors refer to "scriptures" used by "cavemen" in the area of Jericho.

1947

- circa January/February or some indeterminate time before, Bedouin discover three manuscripts in a covered jar in the the first Qumran cave. They remove the scrolls and two jars.

Qumran Cave 4A with two entrances visible on the side and one on top. Cave 4B with one entrance visible to the left. Courtesy of the Israel Antiquities Authority

circa 900-1000

- Al-Qirqisani, a Karaite Jewish historian, refers to a sect of "Magharians," (based on the Arabic word for "cave") "because their books were found in a cave."

March

- Jum'a and Khalil offer the first scrolls to Ibrahim 'Ijha in Bethlehem. These are the Great Isaiah[a] Scroll , the Habakkuk Commentary, and the Manual of Discipline in two pieces.

- Jum'a shows the scrolls to George Isha'ya.

- The scrolls are shown to Kando.

13 April

- Easter Week, according to the Julian Calendar used by branches of the Eastern Orthodox Church, in which Easter may fall one week later than the western calendar. George Isha'ya mentions the scrolls to Mar Athanasius Samuel.

14-21 April

- One week after Orthodox Easter Week, Kando and George bring the Manual of Discipline to the Metropolitan Samuel, the first meeting about scrolls between Kando and Samuel.

May-June

- Jum'a and George return to Cave 1 and remove four more scrolls. Three are sold to Faidi Salahi in Bethlehem. These three are later bought by Sukenik (Isaiah[b], The War Scroll, and The Thanksgiving Scroll). Kando later acquires the fourth one (Genesis Apocryphon).

15 July, Saturday

- Kando sends Jum'a, George and Khalil Musa with four scrolls to St. Mark's, where they are rudely but mistakenly turned away.

5-19 July

- Kando takes four scrolls (in five pieces) on consignment from the Bedouin (Isaiah[a], the Habakkuk Commentary, the Manual of Discipline in two pieces, and the Genesis Apocryphon).

- Two of the original three Bedouin and George Isha'ya return to St. Mark's, but only with the four scrolls now under the control of Kando.

Last week of July

- Fr. Van der Ploeg and Fr. Marmadj from the École Biblique examine the Isaiah scroll (and possibly others) at St. Mark's Monastery in the Old City of Jerusalem, but do not recognize it as ancient. Van der Ploeg informs Samuel that it is the book of Isaiah.

Late July or Early August

- Samuel sends George Isha'ya with Bedouin to the scrolls cave. They report back to Samuel that they found many pieces of cloth wrappings on the cave floor, broken jars and one complete jar.

Second Week of August

- George Isha'ya takes Fr. Yusif from St. Mark's Monastery to visit the scrolls cave. Due to the extreme heat they do not try to carry away the one unbroken jar.

Third Week of August

- Samuel consults Stephan Hanna Stephan, an employee of the Transjordan Department of Antiquities, but Stephan pronounces the scrolls "late."

30 August

- William Brownlee and John Trever arrive in Haifa for a year of study at the American School of Oriental Research in Jerusalem. Director Millar Burrows meets them at the port.

15 September

- Anton Kiraz travels with Mar Samuel to Homs, Syria, north of Damascus, where they show the scrolls to the Afram Barsoum, Patriarch of Antioch for the Syrian Jacobite Church. The Patriarch doubts their antiquity.

22 September
- Metropolitan Mar Athanasius Samuel travels from Syria to Beirut to see the Professor of Hebrew at the American University, but he is away on vacation.

26 September
- Mar Samuel returns to Jerusalem, still having not found anyone who supports the antiquity of the scrolls.

End of September or beginning of October
- Stephan Hanna Stephan brings Toviah Wechsler to examine the scrolls, but he says they are late. Other experts also deny the scrolls' antiquity.

1-3 October
- Anton Kiraz and Mar Samuel become business partners in the scrolls.

Mid-October
- Dr. Maurice Brown sees the scrolls. He calls Judah Magnes, President of the Hebrew University of Jerusalem.

Late October
- President Magnes sends two men from the university library staff to examine the scrolls. Samuel consents to photographs, but the librarians never return.

23 November (Sunday)
- An Armenian antiquities dealer in the Old City of Jerusalem, Nasri Ohan (Mister X in early published accounts), calls Prof. Sukenik and leaves a message. They arrange a meeting for the next day.

24 November (Monday)
- Ohan meets with Sukenik across a barbed wire fence at the gateway to Military Zone B in Jerusalem to see some scraps of parchment with Hebrew script on them. Sukenik [perhaps, actually, Avigad, his assistant] recognizes the script as ancient. Sukenik says he will buy the scraps.

27 November (Thursday)
- The Armenian dealer telephones Sukenik to say he has additional fragments, and they meet in the dealer's shop in the Old City.

28 November (Friday)
- Yadin hears about the scrolls for the first time during a visit to his father's house in Jerusalem. As Chief of Operations of the Haganah, Yadin is aware of the grave danger of violence in Arab areas if the impending United Nations vote on the establishment of a Jewish State is favorable. He joins his mother in recommending that his father not go to Bethlehem to see the scrolls.

29 November (Saturday)
- Sukenik and the Armenian antiquities dealer go by bus to Bethlehem to see Feidi Salahi. They see two of the scrolls jars and two scrolls: the Thanksgiving Scroll and the War Scroll. Sukenik carries the scrolls under his arm on the bus back to Jaffa Gate, and takes them home for inspection.

30 November (Sunday)

• Sukenik decides to buy these scrolls. Later that night the UN votes to partition Palestine. Violence breaks out in the Arab areas of the city.

1 December (Monday)

• Sukenik gets word to his Armenian friend to tell Feidi Salahi that he would buy the scrolls.

Week of December 1-8

• Sukenik hears about the St. Mark's scrolls for the first time from Dr. Magnes, President of the Hebrew University of Jerusalem.

22 December

• Sukenik purchases (from Salahi, through the Armenian Nasri Ohan, Mister X): Isaiah[b] two scroll jars, and possibly some Daniel and other fragments as well.

1948

End of January

• Sukenik receives a letter from Anton Kiraz saying that he wants to show him more scrolls. Sukenik and Kiraz meet at the YMCA in West Jerualem. He takes two scrolls home.

6 February

• Sukenik returns the scrolls to Anton Kiraz at the YMCA. A few days later Sukenik receives word that the Jewish Agency will fund the purchase, but it is too late.

18 February (Wednesday)

• Fr. Sowmy calls Brownlee at the American School but he is gone, so Trever takes the call.

19 February (Thursday)

• At 2:30 p.m. Fr. Sowmy and his brother Ibrahim arrive at the American School and show the scrolls to Trever. The scrolls are later identified as Isaiah[a], the Habakkuk Commentary, the Manual of Discipline (2 pieces), and the Genesis Apocryphon. Trever is able to copy a few lines from Isaiah. Trever recognizes the scrolls' antiquity and identifies it as a copy of Isaiah.

20 February (Friday)

• Trever goes to St. Mark's and persuades Mar Samuel to bring the scrolls back to the American School the next day to be photographed.

21 February (Saturday)

• Trever and Brownlee begin photographing the scrolls. Trever persuades Fr. Sowmy to leave three scrolls for "several days."

Late February or early March

• Trever's photographs arrive at Johns Hopkins University in Baltimore. Prof. Albright shows them to students Frank Moore Cross and David Noel Freedman.

6-11 March

• Scrolls are re-photographed for publication.

15 March

• Trever receives Albright's letter confirming the age of the scrolls.

25 March

• Rev. Butros Sowmy takes the scrolls to Beirut for safekeeping.

March or April

• Sukenik receives a letter from Kiraz and/or Mar Samuel saying they had decided not to sell the scrolls. Only later does he find out the scrolls had been shown to Trever, who had photographed them.

20 April

- In anticipation of the coming war the British High Commissioner of Palestine transfers ownership of the Palestine Archaeological Museum to a newly constituted Board of Trustees. This order is amended on 1 February 1955.

14 May

- The Jewish People's Council declares the independent State of Israel.

15 May

- The British Mandate of Palestine ends and Israel's War of Independence begins.

August

- George Isha'ya visits Cave 1 again and secures some Daniel and Prayer Scroll fragments, which he turns over to Mar Samuel.

November

- Isha'ya, Kando and others excavate Cave 1 and secure many more fragments. This is at least the fourth visit to the cave after the initial discovery.

1949

7 January

- Cease-fire takes effect between Israel and Arab states of the Middle East. Transjordan becomes known as Jordan and controls Qumran, East Jerusalem, the Old City, and the campus of the Hebrew University on Mt. Scopus.

24 January

- Captain Philippe Lippens of Belgium asks

for help from the Arab Legion to re-find the cave, which is accomplished on January 28.

29 January

- Mar Samuel arrives in the United States with four scrolls (Isaiah[a], Habakkuk Commentary, Manual of Discipline, Genesis Apocryphon) and fragments of Daniel, Prayers, and 1 Enoch).

15 February-5 March.

- Cave 1 is excavated under the direction of Harding and de Vaux. Fragments of about seventy scrolls and pieces of fifty pottery jars are recovered.

October

- The St. Mark's scrolls are exhibited at the Library of Congress.

1950

March

- First ASOR volume appears, containing facsimiles of Isaiah[a] and the Habakkuk Commentary.

Spring

- Yusuf Saad succeeds in purchasing the remainder of the Cave 1 fragments in the possession of Kando.

November

- St. Mark's scrolls exhibited at Oriental Institute of the University of Chicago. Carbon-14 test of some of the cloth covers from Cave 1 indicate an age of AD 33 ± 200 years. The results are first published in January 1951.

1951

- De Vaux continues excavations at Qumran.

4 January
- De Vaux is shown fragments from Murabba'at by Bedouin.

21 January-3 March
- Harding and de Vaux interrupt their excavations at Qumran to search the caves at Murabba'at.

March
- ASOR publishes Trever's photographs of the Manual of Discipline from Cave 1.

24 November-12 December
- De Vaux and Harding make soundings at Qumran, confirming the site's connection with Cave 1 through pottery analysis, and establishing the date of the site through coins.

1952

- Caves at Wadi Murabba'at excavated under the direction of de Vaux and Harding.

February
- Cave 2 is discovered to the north of Qumran, near Cave 1.

10-29 March
- Exploration of about 225 caves in the Qumran region, 4 km north and south.
- Cave 3 and the Copper Scroll discovered.

July
- Bedouin discover manuscripts at Khirbet Mird.

July-August
- Bedouin bring to Jerusalem manuscripts from an "unidentified" cave, probably Nahal Hever.

20 September
- Bedouin offer a large number of fragments to the Palestine Archaeological Museum through Kando, and directly, to Père de Vaux at the École Biblique. The government of Jordan pays JD 15,000 ($42,000) for these in early 1953. Harding is immediately notified, and by 3 p.m. a mounted patrol arrives at Qumran and finds the cave. The police leave a guard there.

21 September
- The Department of Antiquities of Jordan, the Palestine Archaeological Museum and the École Biblique prepare themselves for excavating the new cave, Qumran Cave 4.

22-29 September
- Père de Vaux, Milik and others excavate Cave 4, discovering thousands more fragments. Cave 5 is discovered a short distance north of Cave 4 and is excavated by Milik. Shortly after Cave 6 is discovered in a cliff of Wadi Qumran.

Winter 1952-1953

- Kando hides Cave 4 fragments in an inner tube, buries it under the doorway to his house. In the Spring of 1953 he unearths it, only to find that the humidity had reduced all the fragments to jelly.

1953

- E. Sukenik (father of Yadin) dies.

- Bedouin bring Greek Fragments to École Biblique. They turn out to be from Nahal Hever and become known as the Greek Prophets Scroll. The scroll is assigned to Barthélemy for publication.

- Jordanian government pays JD15,000 ($42,000) for Cave 4 fragments.

- An arrangement is reached with the Jordan Government requiring that scroll materials remain in the Palestine Archaeological Museum until prepared for publication, but allowing fragments to go to institutions that donate funds.

February-April
- Khirbet Mird is excavated by R. de Langhe of the University of Louvain, Belgium.

9 February-4 April
- Second season of excavation at Qumran.

Spring
- Harding begins to constitute the Cave 4 Team. Milik and Cross become its first members.

Spring
- Barthélemy falls ill and returns to France.

May
- Cross arrives in Jerusalem.

Summer
- Cross works alone in Jerusalem on the Cave 4 materials excavated by Harding and de Vaux.

September
- Milik arrives back in Jerusalem to begin work on the Cave 4 scrolls.

1954

January
- Starcky joins the Cave 4 Team.

15 February-15 April
- Third excavation season at Qumran.

June
- Skehan joins the Cave 4 Team.

1 June
- Morty Jacobs of New York calls Yadin in Israel to inform him that the St. Mark's scrolls are being advertised for sale in the *Wall Street Journal*.

11 June
- An agreement is reached between Mar Samuel and "Mr. Green" (Prof. Harry Orlinsky) to purchase the scrolls for $250,000. Later that month the purchase is finalized.

Exact month unknown
- Strugnell joins the Cave 4 Team.

1 July
- St. Mark's scrolls are purchased by Yadin in New York on behalf of Israel for $250,000.

October
- Hunzinger joins the Cave 4 Team in Jerusalem for one year, but stays for two.

1955
- The first volume of Discoveries in the Judaean Desert appears from Oxford University Press (Clarendon).

- Controversy begins to swirl around John

Allegro for his statements on the radio and in the popular press.

13 February
- Yadin announces that the St. Mark's scrolls have returned to Jerusalem, to be united with those purchased by his father some years before.

2 February-6 April
- Fourth excavation season at Qumran.
- Caves 7, 8, 9, 10 are discovered in the terraces around Qumran, but yield only small amounts of scroll fragments.

March
- A Hebrew scroll of the Minor Prophets is discovered by Bedouin in a fifth Murabba'at cave

18-29 March
- An Israeli expedition to Masada finds one papyrus document.

Spring
- Publication of *The Dead Sea Scrolls of the Hebrew University* by Sukenik (posthumously, by Avigad and others).

4 October
- In Manchester the last cuts are made of the first part of the Copper Scroll.

14 October
- Allegro tells Harding that his preliminary reading of the Copper Scroll indicates a vast treasure of silver and gold at Qumran.

1956

February

- Bedouin discover Cave 11 and remove all materials, including the Temple Scroll.

7 February
- Announcement in Israel of the unrolling and deciphering of the "Fourth Scroll" (Genesis Apocryphon).

18 February-28 March
- The Excavations at Qumran continue for a fifth and final season. Ain Feshka is also explored.

1 March
- The Palestine Archaeological Museum pays JD 16,000 ($44,800) to Kando for "eight cardboard boxes and one package" of Cave 11 fragments.

Summer
- First gift from McCormick Theological Seminary (Chicago) to purchase Cave 4 scrolls. Cross advises Harding of $6000 available. Harding sends word to Kando that 2100 square centimeters of inscribed material from Cave 4 would be purchased.

circa June
- Gerald Lankester Harding is forcibly removed from his position as Director General of the Department of Antiquities of Jordan. He retains his position with the as yet still private Palestine Archaeological Museum.

17 July
- The Palestine Archaeological Museum pays JD 14,000 ($32,200) for 11Q New Jerusalem and 11Q Targum of Job.

26 July
- Egyptian President Nasser nationalizes the Suez Canal.

October?
- The Cave 4 Team's work is halted owing to the Suez Crisis/Sinai War. All manuscripts and fragments in the Palestine Archaeological Museum are removed to Amman for safekeeping.

11 December
- Strugnell reports to Allegro from London that the Jordanians have now forced Harding out of the Museum as well.

1957

12 February
- First attempt by Jordan to nationalize the scrolls.

4 March
- The scrolls stored in Amman during the Suez Crisis return to Jerusalem.

September
- Some members of the Cave 4 Team view the new Cave 11 material for the first time.

1958

- *Revue de Qumran* founded by Fr. Jean Carmignac (Gabalda, Paris).

25 January-21 March
- Sixth excavation season in Qumran area. Ain Feshka also excavated.

Spring
- Bedouin discover scroll fragments in a cave near En Gedi and bring them to the attention of Israelis.

23 March-6 April
- An Israeli expedition surveys the En Gedi

region, discovering a cave in Nahal Hever with fragments from Psalms, fifteen papyrus letters in Hebrew, Aramaic, and Greek.

June
- Baillet is invited to join the Cave 4 Team.

July
- A second gift from McCormick Theological Seminary (Chicago) and a gift from the All Soul's Unitarian Church (New York) make it possible to purchase the last of the Cave 4 scroll fragments. Others who have made previous Cave 4 purchases possible are: the Federal Government of Bonn and the Government of Baden-Würtemberg on behalf of the University of Heidelberg, McGill University, an unnamed widow, the endowment of the Palestine Archaeological Museum, and the Vatican Library.
- The last fragments from Murabba'at are purchased by the Palestine Archaeological Museum and the École Biblique.

1959

March
- Nahal Hever is further excavated by Israeli archaeologists.

1960

- On behalf of the American Schools Cross negotiates the purchase of the Cave 11 Psalms Scroll.

- The Royal Netherlands Academy of Sciences acquires publication rights to the Cave 11 Job Targum.

- The Rockefeller funds supporting the work of the Cave 4 Team are discontinued.

Early in the year

- Rumors that many fragments brought to Jerusalem by Bedouin had come from Nahal Se'elim results in a survey of the valley by Aharoni. Documentary fragments are found only in one cave.

23 March-6 April

- Yadin excavates the Cave of Letters (Cave 5/6) in Nahal Hever.

1961

Spring

- Murabba'at manuscripts and artifacts are published as DJD 2.

14-27 March

- Yadin mounts a second expedition to Nahal Hever.

5 August

- The Hashemite Kingdom of Jordan revokes all past agreements concerning eventual transfer of scrolls to donors who provided funds for their purchase from the Bedouin. The government nationalizes the scrolls, claiming absolute ownership.

10-20 November

- Psalms scroll from Cave 11 opened by Sanders.

1962

February

- Bedouin discover about forty papyrus documents (known as the Samaria papyri), dating to the 4th century B.C., in a large

cave in Wadi ed-Daliyeh, about nine miles north of Jericho.

March

- Fragments of an Ezekiel scroll from Cave 11 recovered. It is later assigned to Brownlee for study.

Fall

- Publication of DJD 3, describing fragments and artifacts from Caves 2, 3, 5-10.

14 November

- Cross arrives in Jerusalem on behalf of the American Schools with $20,000 to buy the papyri from Wadi ed-Daliyeh.

15 November

- De Vaux, Saad, Cross, and Prof. and Mrs. Paul Lapp meet with Kando to negotiate for the papyri, finally buying all of it for more than $30,000.

19 November

- Cross and the Lapps unroll the papyri at the Museum.

October through April 1964

- Excavators working under Yadin at Masada discover fragments of many manuscripts, including Hebrew, Greek, and Latin documents. Escavations continue December 1964-March 1965.

1965

- Cross begins negotiating for the purchase of publication rights for the 11Q Paleo-Hebrew Leviticus scroll on behalf of ASOR for $23,000. The negotiation is suspended the following year when the Palestinian Archaeological Museum is nationalized by Jordan.

- Fr. Benoît takes over from Fr. de Vaux as Director of the École Biblique.

1966

6 August
- The Hashemite Kingdom of Jordan nationalizes the Palestine Archaeological Museum.

3 March
- Cross travels from the US to Jerusalem and then Beirut to negotiate with Kando for additional Cave 11 material.

11 March
- Kando shows Cross several boxes of fragments, some from Cave 11, others from the Bar Kokhba era. He offers a "large scroll," later known as the Temple Scroll, but does not have it with him.

4 June
- The Six-Day War begins.

6 June
- Israeli troops capture the Palestine Archaeological Museum. They find the scrolls packed for shipment, still in the Museum.

8 June
- Yadin sends soldiers to Kando's home in Bethlehem. They force him to hand over the Temple Scroll, an unprecedented seizure of private property.

1968

- Allegro publishes his texts in DJD 5. Strugnell replies with a scathing 118 page review.

1971

September
- Fr. Roland de Vaux dies.

Winter 1971-72
- Baillet returns again to Jerusalem to work on his texts with the support of the CNRS. The Scrollery in the Palestine Archaeological Museum (now the Rockefeller Museum) has been completely dismantled by Israelis, and the texts moved to the basement. Baillet finds the manuscripts "damaged." Other texts are simply missing, having been on a "world tour," but never having "returned to the fold." Some of these never show up again (according to Baillet, 1982). The concordances are in disorder in the bottoms of cupboards and there is no photographic department.

1972

- Benoît is appointed to be de Vaux's successor and is able to conclude an agreement with "all parties" involved in the scrolls (presumably the Department of Antiquities of Israel, the Cave 4 Team, and Oxford University Press) to continue the publication of DJD.

1974

- Fr. Starcky appoints Fr. Emile Puech to take over the publication of his fragments.

August
- Due to an unspecified disagreement between the Department of Antiquities of

Israel and the Cave 4 Team, work ceases on publication of the scrolls.

1975

May
• Work on the publication of the scrolls resumes.

1977

• Publication of DJD 6, containing a summary of Qumran Archaeology by de Vaux and the edition of Cave 4 texts 128-157 by Milik.

1980

• Strugnell attempts to persuade Oxford University Press to publish in fascicles those sections of each editor's work that were then ready in final form, but the Press' Mr. Cordy does not agree.

• Barthélemy turns over his notes on the Greek Minor Prophets scroll to Emanuel Tov and gives him the responsibility of publishing it in DJD.

• The first woman (Carol Newsom) is assigned to the scrolls team by Strugnell.

1982

• Baillet's volume is published as DJD 7. His manuscript was ready six years before.

1984

• 28 June, Yigael Yadin dies in Hadara, Israel at the age of 67.

1985

• Strugnell is appointed editor in chief of DJD.

1986

• Strugnell's appointment as editor in chief is confirmed by the Israel Department of Antiquities. In the interval between Benoit's retirement in 1984 and Strugnell's confirmation in 1986, Mrs. Bechtel loses patience and withdraws her promised contribution of $300,000 ($350,000?) to the Cave 4 Publication Team.

April-May and 22-23 June
• H. Eshel excavates Wadi el-Mafjar discovering 4th century BC and 2nd century BC Aramaic and Greek documents.

1987

• Strugnell secures some funding from a Jewish donor in England to help with the preparations of texts for DJD.

23 April 1987
• Fr. Pierre Benoît, O.P., dies in Jerusalem at the age of 81. He had lived in Jerusalem for fifty-five years.

1988

• Tov publishes Vol. 8 of the DJD, the Greek Minor Prophets Scroll.
• Fr. Jean Starcky dies

17 February
• Allegro suffers a sudden heart attack, and dies on his 65th birthday.

1990

Mid-November

- Prof. Strugnell is relieved of his duties as editor in chief by the oversight committee of the Israel Antiquities Authority.

- Prof. Emanuel Tov of the Hebrew University of Jerusalem is appointed in Strugnell's place.

1991

14-15 January

- Tov and Weston Fields meet in Paris. They discuss the organization of the scrolls team and Tov invites Fields to the Madrid Conference.

March

- The Madrid Conference at which Tov asks Fields for ideas about funding the publication of the scrolls. Preliminary plans are made for the formation of the Dead Sea Scrolls Foundation.

May

- Tov and Fields meet at the Netherlands Institute of Advanced Study in Wassenaar and formalize plans for the Dead Sea Scrolls Foundation, including choosing candidates for the Board of Directors and Board of Advisors.

September

- The Huntington Library (California) releases illegally obtained photographs of scrolls. These are published by Hershel Shanks and James Robinson.

1992

November

- At the SBL Annual Meeting in San Francisco, the Dead Sea Scrolls Foundation holds its first meeting, appointing Weston Fields as Executive Director. Board members are Cross, Fitzmyer, Greenfield, Harrelson, Kraft, Meyers, Sanders, Talmon, Tov (chairperson), and Ulrich.

1992/1993

- Tov persuades Oxford University Press to allow the publication of DJD volumes out of order, making it possible to publish the volumes as they are ready.

1993

- Publication of the Dead Sea Scrolls on Microfiche by publishers E. J. Brill and IDC in the Netherlands.

1994

November

- H. Eshel discovers Aramaic documents from the Bar-Kokhba period on an upper shelf of a cave near Jericho.

1995

- Publication of *The Dead Sea Scrolls Translated* by Florentino García Martínez (Brill), the most complete English translation up to the time.

1997

- Publication of the Dead Sea Scrolls CD-ROM by Brill.

1999

Summer

- Martin Schøyen, a collector in Norway and a member of the Dead Sea Scrolls Foundation Board of Advisors, obtains two unpublished scroll fragments, one of Joshua and one of Judges.

2002

- Tov resigns as chairperson of the Dead Sea Scrolls Foundation, but remains on the board of directors and its executive committee. Prof. Shalom Paul from the Hebrew University of Jerusalem assumes duties as chairperson.

10 February

- Fr. D. Bartélemy, O.P., dies in Fribourg, Switzerland.

2003

- Publication of the first part off the Dead Sea Scrolls Concordance by Brill.

2004

4 August

- Fr. Van der Ploeg dies in Nijmegen, the Netherlands.

2005

January

- Cross finishes his work on 4Q Samuel, published later in the year as DJD 17.

21 November

- The Dead Sea Scrolls Electronic Library (Brill/ISPART) is demonstrated at the Society of Biblical Literature Annual Meeting in Philadelphia.

2006

6 January

- Milik dies in Paris.

Dead Sea region. © Roi Zaka; Mantsur/Shutterstock

GLOSSARY

ASOR: American Schools of Oriental Research. The Jerusalem school was later known as the Albright Institute of Archaeology.

Apocrypha: The books included in the Septuagint but not in the Hebrew Bible. Some of these books are included in the Catholic and Orthodox Bibles, but are excluded from Protestant Bibles.

Apocryphon: A book which consists of expansion of a biblical book. Among the Dead Sea Scrolls, the Genesis Apocryphon is an example.

Aramaic: A language closely related to Hebrew, which was the common language of the Middle East from about the 6th century BCE, and a prominent language during the lifetime of Jesus. Many of the Dead Sea Scrolls are written in Aramaic. Several dialects are still spoken, and Syriac, "Christian Aramaic" is still used by the Syrian Orthodox and Catholic churches.

BCE: Before the Common Era, equivalent to BC in the Christian calendar.

Canon: Collection of writings deemed sacred and therefore part of the Bible.

CE: The Common Era, equivalent to AD in the Christian calendar.

Codex: A book with pages in contrast to a scroll.

DAJ: Department of Antiquities of Jordan.

Essenes: An ancient Jewish sect known from Josephus. Most scholars identify the group at Qumran as Essenes.

First Temple: The Temple built by Solomon

in Jerusalem about 950 BCE, destroyed by the Babylonians in 586 BCE.

IAA: Israel Antiquities Authority.

Khirbet: Arabic word for a mound of ruins at an ancient occupation site.

LXX: Septuagint, the Greek translation of the Hebrew Old Testament.

Masada: The fortress built by Herod the Great on a self-standing mountain about midway down the western shore of the Dead Sea. It was occupied by some of the last hold-outs of the First Jewish Revolt and destroyed by the Romans in 73 A.D. after approximately 900 people committed suicide rather than surrender. During its excavation in the 1960s some scrolls were found, which are also included among the "Dead Sea Scrolls."

Masoretic Text: The traditional Hebrew text of the Bible (Old Testament).

New Testament: The 27 books produced by early Christians and combined with the Old Testament to form the Christian Bible.

Old Testament: The traditional Christian term for the Jewish Hebrew Bible. The term is used to refer to Bibles both with and without the Apocrypha.

Ostracon: A piece of broken pottery with writing on it.

Paleography: The comparative study of ancient handwriting styles in order to date ancient documents.

PAM: Palestine Archaeological Museum, now the Rockefeller Museum, in Jerusalem.

Pesher: A type of interpretation of biblical books found among the Dead Sea Scrolls which understands the Bible in terms of the recent past, present, and near future of the sect at Qumran.

Qumran: Archaeological site near NW corner of the Dead Sea, close to 11 caves in which scrolls were discovered.

Second Temple: Rebuilt Jerusalem Temple; time period roughly 500 BCE to 70 CE.

Septuagint: The Greek translation of the Hebrew Bible traditionally begun at approximately 250 BCE in Alexandria. It also includes some of the books of the "Apocrypha," and was the Bible of Greek-speaking Jews and the Old Testament of Greek-speaking Christians for centuries.

Ta'amireh: Tribe of Bedouin, some of whom found the first Dead Sea Scrolls

Wadi: Arabic word for a dry riverbed in the desert, which is seasonally filled with water during the rainy season, usually during flash floods. Equivalent to Hebrew *nahal*.

Yahad: Hebrew word meaning "group," used of themselves by the Qumranites.

Dead Sea region. © Roi Zaka; Mantsur/Shutterstock

SUGGESTIONS FOR FURTHER STUDY

Editions

Abegg, M. G., Jr., Bowley, J., Cook, E., and Tov, E. *The Dead Sea Scrolls Concordance*, 2 vols. Leiden: Brill, 2003.

Discoveries in the Judaean Desert, 37 vols. Oxford University Press, 1955-present.

García Martínez, F. and Tigchelaar, E. J. C. *The Dead Sea Scrolls Study Edition,* 2 vols. Leiden: Brill, 1998.

Parry, D. and Tov, E. *The Dead Sea Scrolls Reader.* Leiden: Brill, 2004/2005.

Tov, E., with the collaboration of S. J. Pfann. *The Dead Sea Scrolls on Microfiche: A Comprehensive Facsimile Edition of the Texts from the Judean Desert, with a Companion Volume.* Leiden: Brill and IDC, 1995.

Translations

Abegg, M. G., Jr., Flint, P. W. and Ulrich, E. C. The *Dead Sea Scrolls Bible: The Oldest Known Bible Translated for the First Time into English*. San Francisco: Harper, 1999.

García Martínez, F. *The Dead Sea Scrolls Translated*. The Qumran texts in English. Leiden: Brill, 1994.

Vermes, G. *The Complete Dead Sea Scrolls in English*, Revised and extended 4th Edition. London: Penguin, 1995.

General Works

Burrows, M. *The Dead Sea Scrolls.* New York: The Viking Press, 1955.

Davies, P. R., Brooke, G. J., and Callaway, P. R. *The Complete World of the Dead Sea Scrolls.* London: Thames and Hudson, 2002.

Cross, F. M., Jr. *The Ancient Library of Qumran and Modern Biblical Studies.* Grand Rapids: Baker Book House, reprint 1980.

Fitzmeyer, J. A. *Responses to 101 Questions on the Dead Sea Scrolls.* New York: Paulist Press, 1992.

Flint, P. W. and VanderKam, J. C. *The Meaning of the Dead Sea Scrolls: Their Significance for Understanding the Bible, Judaism, Jesus, and Christianity.* New York: Harper Collins, 2002.

Magness, J. *The Archaeology of Qumran and the Dead Sea Scrolls.* Grand Rapids: Eerdmans, 2003.

Mébarki, F and Puech, E. *Les manuscripts de la Mer Morte.* Paris: Editions Rouergue, 2002.

Milik, J. T. *Ten Years of Discovery in the Wilderness of Judaea.* SCM Press, 1959.

Price, R. *Secrets of the Dead Sea Scrolls.* Eugene: Harvest House, 1996.

Schiffman, L. *Reclaiming the Dead Sea Scrolls: The History of Judaism, the background of Christianity, the lost library of Qumran.* New York: Doubleday, 1994.

Stegemann, H. *The Library of Qumran.* Grand Rapids: Eerdmans, Brill, 1998.

Trever, J. C. *Dead Sea Scrolls in Perspective.* North Richland Hills, TX: Bibal Press, 2004.

Ulrich, E. *The Dead Sea Scrolls and the Origins of the Bible.* Grand Rapids: Eerdmans and Brill, 1999.

VanderKam, J. C. *Dead Sea Scrolls Today.* Grand Rapids: Eerdmans, 1998.